Your One W...
to Mind-F...

John O'Keeffe has used mind-fitness to achieve both
business and personal success. He became a hockey
international at 19 and his own boss at 21.
He taught himself Mandarin and has travelled all over
the world. At 38 he became managing director
of Procter & Gamble, famous for brands such as
Ariel, Pampers, Fairy Liquid, Daz, Flash
and many others.

Your One Week Way to Mind-Fitness

John O'Keeffe

Thorsons
An Imprint of HarperCollins*Publishers*

Thorsons
An Imprint of HarperCollins*Publishers*
77–85 Fulham Palace Road,
Hammersmith, London W6 8JB
1160 Battery Street,
San Francisco, California 94111-1213

Published by Thorsons 1994
10 9 8 7 6 5 4 3 2 1

© John O'Keeffe 1994

John O'Keeffe asserts the moral right to
be identified as the author of this work

A catalogue record for this book
is available from the British Library

ISBN 0 7225 2925 2

Phototypeset by
Harper Phototypesetters Limited,
Northampton, England
Printed in Great Britain by
HarperCollinsManufacturing Glasgow

This book is dedicated to
Jeannie, Tim, Sam and Kelly,
who I hope can use this knowledge
better than I have.

Contents

Day 1

What Good Mind-food Can do for You, in a Week

What's in This Book for You?

Are you thinking there is nothing in this book for you? Well, can you see anything in Figure 1 or does it just seem to be a collection of meaningless marks?

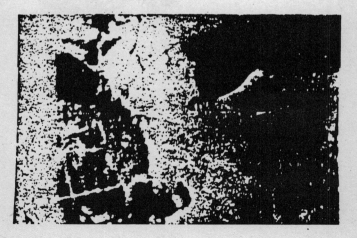

Figure 1

Do the shapes in Figure 2 mean anything to you?

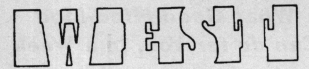

Figure 2

Or those in Figure 3?

Figure 3

What are the lines in Figure 4? Are they anything sensible or not? Look at them closely.

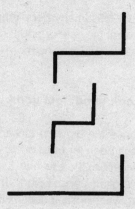

Figure 4

Nothing in these? Perhaps you've decided already that you can't see anything in one or two of them. Well, you'd be wrong and at the end of this chapter there is an explanation as to why. There *is* something in each of these pictures, once you 'see' it.

In the same way, you'd be completely wrong if you thought there was nothing in this book for you. It's absolutely right for you. There are more than 200 ideas and exercises, and if you can 'see' how to apply just 20 of them, your life will be substantially happier and more fulfilling, more fun – and so will the lives of those around you. Don't prejudge this book like you might have prejudged that 'you just can't see' those pictures.

You can, once you are told how.

What Big Idea Do You Need to 'See' in This Book?

Since the 1970s and 1980s, many people have started being more careful about what they eat or about how much alcohol they drink. People have started taking more exercise. The idea has been:

Look good, feel good.

For some, this has meant a big step forward in the quality of their lives, but it hasn't been for most of us. We either couldn't keep up the diet or keep up the exercise. It all just didn't seem worth it. Moreover, it often doesn't work. It doesn't help you succeed in what you want in life. It doesn't help in how happy you feel in your job or in your relationships. It doesn't help remove your worries or your frustrations. It doesn't stop you sometimes feeling fed-up with life.

Now people are beginning to realize that the most important fitness we need isn't body fitness, it is '*mind-fitness*'. This is the real key to our quality of life. The 'ideas' are:

Think well, succeed well.
Think good, feel good.

The thoughts in our minds and how we deal with them are what make our days and life successful or unsuccessful, happy or unhappy. Our thoughts can limit us in solving our problems or can give us the thrill of a new idea that helps things. They can limit us to our old ways or open up new ways to get what we want out of life. They can make us feel great or feel lousy. Feel energetic or feel tired. Feel stimulated or feel depressed. Feel in a good mood or feel in a bad mood. Feel life is good or feel life is a pain.

Moreover, human beings are the only animals that can consciously decide to *choose* what and how to think, the mind-set to have or the mood to adopt. All other animals act on automatic.

What's more, it's easy! No difficult keep-fit classes we can never keep up with. No diet instructions that seem to cause us to lose the pleasures in life. Mind-fitness is easy – everyone can do it – and without much effort. The results are fast too! Tomorrow, you can get great ideas to help you move ahead in what you want. Tomorrow, you can feel great.

Mind-fitness is to do with avoiding the mind-sets that restrict our ability to find better ideas. It is to do with avoiding the unnecessary thoughts that cause our bad moods and cause us to feel lousy. It is to do with *choosing* what to think about and how to think about it and be in good moods versus bad ones, have great days versus off-days and feel 'high' more often than 'low'. When we feel good, we get much more done, get much more satisfaction and bring much more joy and fun to those around us.

The Big Idea you need to 'see' is that you can get more out of life, more out of yourself and bring more happiness to those around you by paying more attention to 'mind-food' and your 'mind-diet' than you regularly do to body-food and body-diet. The thoughts we feed our minds are mind-food. Recall the phrase 'food for thought' and realize how stimulating are the situations in which that phrase has applied for you. There is also 'food for mood' which can be equally stimulating. *Good* mind-food makes us creative, it makes us feel good. *Bad* mind-food makes us 'stuck', makes us feel lousy. A mind-diet is a way to plan what sort of good mind-food we will eat and what bad mind-food we will avoid.

You can plan your mind-food and diet in just the same way as you decide what body-food will make up your body-diet, as follows.

Mealtimes

Three times a day – mealtimes – we think quite carefully what food to feed our bodies. We choose our favourite cereal, our juice, coffee with sugar or no sugar, milk or no milk at breakfast, for example. We plan recipes. We shop to choose food for each of our meals. Indeed, much time is spent on planning meals and shopping for them.

Yet, never on a regular basis do most of us think about what thoughts we put into our minds at 'mealtimes'. In fact, we even consider what body-food we *don't* want to feed into our body, because it's bad for us or gives us indigestion or, simply, we know we just don't like it. Yet, how often do we consider what thoughts we do not want to entertain, because they tend to make us 'down' or what thoughts we would like to feed into our minds instead that would help us enjoy life more. Shouldn't we plan three mind-mealtimes a day, too? Shouldn't we, three times a day, choose our mind-food with at least as much care as we choose our body-food?

Food When Thinking and Influencing Others

When we are in a situation where we need to think or influence others we think about body-food as stimulants too much, even more than we think of mind-food. Thus, in a meeting, we will offer coffee and biscuits. To do business, we invite people to lunch or to dinner to talk and spend time and energy on finding the right place, serving the right food. We may say, 'Let's go for a drink and discuss it.' On our own, we give ourselves cups of coffee or trips to the water fountain when we want to think.

By contrast, too few of us consider what food we might give

our *minds* to help with the problem – to open up our minds from our previous mind-sets – or indeed, mind-food to open up the other person's mind. We know that our opinions, our biases and our prejudices will get in the way, but we feed our minds little to change it. Nor do we offer mind-food to others to help them change their mind-sets. We accept the ideas we have and spend more time arguing and defending them than we do thinking of new ideas to make things better. (Days 2 and 3 will tell you how to improve your mind-fitness and do this.)

Snacking

For our bodies, we often think what to eat and what not to eat between meals. Sometimes it's just 'Don't eat that or you'll spoil your appetite.' Sometimes we're on a diet and will deliberately resist things like crisps, peanuts or chocolate and seek out things like apples. In other situations we really will get pleasure by giving ourselves a snack. We think, 'What do I really fancy right now?' and if the answer is a cream cake, perhaps you give yourself a cream cake or a chocolate bar. The point is that we actually think about what to feed our bodies between meals – either to give us pleasure via the fun of eating snacks we really adore or to give us the pleasure of resisting all snack food as part of an overall plan to lose weight and look better or to get pleasure by choosing a particular snack food that is both enjoyable and healthy.

By direct contrast, too few of us actually think about what to allow our minds to eat and feed on between meals. Our thoughts are just dictated by whatever comes into our heads at any particular moment. If something happens to trigger a bad thought, we just leave it there and entertain it. We just react. We focus on the thought our mind alights on even if we don't want that thought in the first place. It is rather like listening to a radio that will stop at a station that has a strong signal and we leave it on that station even though it is not the one we're looking for. We do not press the button and move on to the station we actually want.

There are ways to avoid just grazing through the cupboard and, in the same way, there are means of avoiding the sort of mind-snack food that we don't really want. There are ways of recognizing when our radio is stopping at a station that's completely uninteresting and unhelpful and moving it on to a station that will give us fun, achievement and satisfaction. (Day 4 will tell you how to do this.)

Morning Exercises

There is great emphasis on doing some sort of exercise first thing to keep fit and get the day off to a good start. What most of us would find more helpful, though, would be morning mind-fitness exercises and ways in which to plan how to have a nice day as opposed to it being a mere accident of fate whether we have one or not. Far better than physical jerks to help the body feel good would be mind-jerks to help our mind feel good, get the day off to a good start and keep it that way. Treat today as though you're in a holiday mood. It is the first day of the rest of your life; make it a special one. (The chapter Day 5 will tell you how to do this.)

Social Food

We think about food for our bodies, perhaps for our guests, when we meet people: 'Can I ask you out to dinner?' 'Would you like to come round for something to eat?', 'We need to go to Grandma's for Sunday lunch.' When someone calls round, we ask them 'Can I get you a cup of coffee, tea, a soft drink? Would you like a biscuit?' We focus on food for the body. In a situation where we ask somebody round for dinner, we spend much energy planning the menu. This is a regular part of our social interaction.

Again, however, we don't spend enough time on what food we will give our mind in these situations. Often the food we are going to give our mind is going to be far, far, more important to getting to know the person better and getting on with them better, than the food we decide to give our bodies. Apart from it being 'a nice meal' and part of a sense of hospitality, the food we give our bodies will actually make very little contribution to a relationship.

On the other hand, when we know we are going for lunch at the grandparents' house and that the last five times we've done this it ended up in family rows, the food we feed our minds before this visit and the food we feed our minds during it is going to be far more important than the food we are feeding our bodies. The way we allow our mind to react the first time a provocative remark is made is far more important in deciding how successful the visit will be than any body-food. We want the visit to be a success, but we don't take the necessary action to feed our mind the right food to make it one and hope that food for the body will achieve it.

The same is true in all our social interactions. To make them a success, we need to sit down to give our mind the right food to help achieve that success. In other words have a nice thought as well as a nice cup of tea. (Day 5 will tell you how to do this.)

What to Eat Arriving Home from Work

The transition from work to home is difficult for both partners in a relationship. Both for the person who has been in a work-type environment going home partly with a view to rest and recuperate; and for the person receiving the other back into their domain, with its different problems and different day.

Once again, our practice is often to think about food for the body as the best way to achieve this transition. Sometimes, it is having a drink on the way home or a drink while preparing the evening meal and a drink and a nibble on arrival or, simply looking forward to the evening meal.

Far more important, however, is the food we give our minds as this will make the first few seconds or minutes constructive ones. Just a few bad words or a few misinterpreted signals can lead to the mind concluding that the other person is in a bad mood or the other person has put you in a bad mood and then there goes the whole evening. This happens simply because we do not pay as much attention to our mind-food as body-food, and it happens time after time. (Day 6 will tell you how to eat good mind-food, both of you, on the arrival home from work.)

Weighing Yourself and Planning Your Mind-diet

Several times a year most of us decide we'll go on a diet. These can be one-week diets, one-month diets or last even longer. The point is that we plan in advance what we will and what we won't give our bodies. We measure our progress regularly by weighing ourselves – probably daily or at least weekly.

Too few of us actually decide on a 'mind-diet', which is when we plan in advance what to feed our minds. Yet, what our minds think is what determines our success, our mood and how good life is for us. We'll benefit more from a mind-diet than a body-diet. We should 'weigh' ourselves regularly to see how good our mind-fitness is. (Day 7 will tell you how to do this.)

The key habit we need to develop is to think of food for our mind as often as we consider food for our body – both what will be bad for us and what will be good for us; what we'll enjoy and what we won't.

18

It's a good practice to notice how often we think of what to feed our bodies and to get into the habit of noting each time we think of this and then thinking of good and bad food for our minds.

Notice your 10 Bad Mind-food Habits

Outlined below are 10 bad mind-food habits. How many of them do you have? You probably don't have all of them and certainly don't have all of them all of the time, but just having a couple, some of the time, can really affect the quality of your success, your moods and the quality of your life. It is likely that you will exhibit all of them to some degree some of the time. Decide today to notice how often your mind has one of these habits.

If you can just change a few of these habits from bad to good for at least part of the time, this book will have changed your life, for the better. Good mind-food can change each and every one of these habits. At the end of this chapter, fill in the short quiz of habits. By the end of this book, do it again and you should be scoring far higher.

Bad Habit 1: You Act Closed-minded

Perhaps not on everything, all of the time, but on some subjects some of the time. You think you are not biased or prejudiced, but you are. You consider yourself open-minded, but, in fact, you have a fairly closed mind on some things, often in a restricting way.

On some subjects you just can't accept a different point of view than your own. You are sure you are 'right'. You tend to reject different points of view as being not as good as yours.

You reject suggestions on how to do things differently because you are sure your way is best. You think it's soundly based on 'experience' or 'on the facts'.

You believe you do not have fixed mind-sets. It is clear this is right and that is wrong. Often you think that there is nothing in other people's suggestions or opinions. You think things are clear from the facts. You think that it's changing other people's mind-sets that's the problem.

Much of the food you feed your mind simply reinforces your attitude or your opinion. You select food or 'facts' that reinforce your ingrained attitude and so miss the opportunity to improve your success and your life through new and different ideas.

The Good Habit
This book will teach you some good mind-food for recognizing when you have 'mind-sets' that are restricting your ability to perform the best action for achieving what you want. It will also give you food to help others open their minds.

Good mind-food can stop the first bad habit of acting closed-minded.

Bad Habit 2: Accept There Can't be a Better Idea
Some things, you think, just can't be better, even though you want them to be – it's just the way things are. You accept things as 'facts of life' even when they restrict you. You are not creative in solving your problems and getting more out of life.

You accept the first answer to a problem, rather than seeking something better. Often you will spend more time arguing why your idea is right than you will looking for something better. Most of your ideas are based on your previous mind-sets and you rarely act on new ideas. Some things you are so sure won't work that you don't even try them. Some things just 'can't be done' and you're so sure that you spend little thought on how they *could* be done.

The Good Habit
Good mind-food can help you to question the solutions that limit you, search for better answers and focus on new ideas to help you achieve what you want.

Good mind-food can stop the second bad habit of thinking that there can't be a better idea.

Bad Habit 3: No Daily Diet – You Just 'Graze'
The mood you have is determined by what comes into your mind. It can be triggered by anything and once the thought is in, you entertain it, even if it makes you grumpy, worried or unhappy and, therefore, ineffective. Very rarely do thoughts 'just happen' that delight you. In fact, most of the time, thoughts come in that make you feel a little 'down'.

This can be due to something someone said, something someone did or didn't do, how someone reacted to you, something that needs doing, something you wished you'd done differently, something that's unfair, something that needs fixing, something that puts you in a rush, puts you behind or gives you worry. Overall the thought puts you in a poorer mood than you were.

This is caused by 'grazing'. It's like the person who chooses what to eat by seeing what's in the cupboard and ends up eating crisps, biscuits, peanuts and other snacks all the time or sheep grazing in a field, mindlessly eating what's in front of them or a spider eating whatever comes into its web. More than anything it's like a modern radio that has a scanner button. You're on 'scan'. The radio simply stops and con-centrates when it receives a signal. It could be a station in German or Czech or French or whatever. It can also be an unclear signal with lots of static and interference. Grazing in the mind is the equivalent of stopping and listening to it, just because it's there. Because the thought 'came to me' just like a lousy programme came on the scanner radio.

The Good Habit

This book will teach you to simply press the scan button again and 'move on' rather than dwell on really unnecessary thoughts that don't help you. Moreover, it will help you plan in advance some 'good stations' that you enjoy and will teach you how to tune in to these.

Good mind-food can stop the bad habit of 'just grazing' and can create a good habit in its place.

Bad Habit 4: You Have a 'Bad Day'

Do you have days that go from bad to worse?

A man wakes up early. Fifteen minutes too early. Regrets it, feels he hasn't had quite enough sleep and so feels tired. Comes down to breakfast. His wife makes an unexpected request from him to remember something that day. He snaps. She snaps back. They argue. He leaves the house with a polite peck. Goes to buy his paper. His mind is elsewhere. The newspaper seller gruffly asks him what he wants. He feels annoyed at the seller's attitude. Turns round, someone bumps into him. Doesn't say sorry. The train is a couple of minutes late. He gets a bit angry about this but spends the time going over the scene with his wife. Sees the person on the platform who bumped into him. Feels angry. He looks the sort who wouldn't care about manners. On the train, he feels someone unfairly got the seat he should have had. By the time he gets to work it's already 'a bad day'. He gets upset at the first 'bad' thing. The people around him think that's unfair and react accordingly. He insists. By now he's feeling physically bad –

he has a bit of a headache. He doesn't handle things as diplomatically as he normally would so people react to this and there are some arguments. So it continues.

By the end of the day, he is absolutely shattered. He is in no state to repair the relationship at home. He comes in, wants to do nothing but eat and slump in front of the TV because 'he's had a bad day'. The last thing he's ready to do is put energy into explaining to his wife what went wrong or apologize for snapping. His wife, though, remembers the snapping and now, after a bad day, they are heading for a bad evening.

Why Does It Happen?

Because entertaining one negative thought, having one piece of bad mind-food, leads to feeling bad, which leads to interpreting the next event negatively and so on. The negative thought leads to a negative mood, then you react negatively and people react to that accordingly.

The mind is eating no different food that might change the mood and thus change the action and reaction so a vicious circle is created.

The Good Habit

Far better is to give the mind some mind-food to stop the day going so badly. This can be done at any stage, just like good food:

- we can do it before the day starts by deciding the night before to 'get out on the right side of bed' the next day rather than let it just be dictated by the first random thought your mind receives when it wakes up
- we can decide at breakfast how to 'have a good day'
- we can have good mind-food snacks

- we can decide the mind-food to go home on, rather than let the evening be decided by what greets us when we get through the door.

Good mind-food can stop the fourth bad habit of *allowing* yourself to have a bad day and can create a good habit in its place.

Bad Habit 5: Once You Remember One Thing Bad, You Remember Others

This habit can take all shapes:

- Your partner does something that is a bad habit and it annoys you. You immediately allow your mind to trigger all the other 'bad' things about your partner. It doesn't need to be your partner, however, it can be something your mother does that really irritates you, something the children keep on doing, something your boss does. Suddenly one thing leads to another and you have a real dislike of that person.
- Why don't the children turn that radio down? They're always having it blast away! They're getting more and more inconsiderate. Do you know yesterday they also, etc., etc. They can't possibly do their homework well with it on. They won't get the grades they need. I saw their homework books last week and they really didn't show much care and attention.

  What's happening? You are allowing your mind-thoughts to drift on to *all* the bad things triggered by one thing that you interpreted in a bad way – the radio noise.
- Your husband has gone to work and the day was going to be good, that is until you went upstairs and found his clothes all over the floor. Who does he think you are, a charwoman, picking up after him all the time? The cupboard door is left

open again. Why does he leave it for you to shut? The bath needing cleaning. Why can't he do it himself? By the time this train of thought has started you're also remembering how fat he is now, how his breath sometimes smells, how he slumps in front of the TV – indeed, how unlovable he is.

Why Does it Happen?

You are allowing your mind-thoughts to drift on to all the bad things triggered by just one thing that you interpreted in a bad way.

You are feeding your mind bad mind-food and just continuing to nibble at it without thinking. If he knew you were going to think all those bad things about him, do you think he would ever have left his clothes on the floor in the first place?

Once started on a negative train of thought, your thoughts continue to drift in the negative. There is nothing positive put into your mind to trigger a train of all the wonderful things about him – the small things he does, the fun he is, the experiences you've shared, how sexy he can be. There is no good mind-food to stop you continuing to nibble away at the junk-food you've started eating.

The Good Habit

Decide in advance some positive anchors about the people in your life that you ask your mind to focus on when it starts drifting to the bad ones.

- Identify, list and remember all the virtues and good points of your children. Think of all the ways they are likeable. Think of the great fun occasions you've had together.
- Spend some minutes thinking of all the good things about your partner, now and in the past. Picture them. Smile. Remember any special music between you.

When you find your mind drifting to bad thoughts, switch it to the channel of remembering the good things. Do this at the same time as doing something physically. Run upstairs for example, whilst switching. In this way balance easily returns and you'll be out of your disabling mood.

Good mind-food can stop the fifth bad habit of once remembering one bad thing, remembering others and can create a good habit in its place.

Bad Habit 6: Allow the Wrong Frame of Reference to Occur

Picture yourself in a railway carriage on a long journey. You've been quite looking forward to enjoying the journey. You bought some newspapers, a good book and have one or two things to do. You start getting increasingly distracted and annoyed by a family of children further up the carriage who are beginning to misbehave. They are loud, noisy, occasionally yelling. They have started running around. They're with their mother, who doesn't seem to be doing enough to control them in your view. She encourages them to sit down but when they don't obey her she only half-heartedly scolds them. You are getting annoyed at this, both at the behaviour of the children and at the behaviour of the mother. You can't concentrate on your book, you can't concentrate on your papers, you're getting exasperated. You're making remarks to your partner about how bad these kids are and you pass on to each other the next example of bad behaviour. All in all it's getting quite intolerable. You're wondering whether you should get up and complain. You don't want to, but, on the other hand, you think you should. These kids are ruining the day for you.

Then, suddenly, the mother walks down the railway carriage towards you, stops by you and says, 'I'm really sorry about the way the children are behaving, because I think it's annoying you and I can understand that. They have had a bad shock. This morning I had to take them to the hospital where my husband was dying of cancer, for him to say goodbye to them. He died while they were there. I'm now taking them to my mother's to stay for a few days. Overall, they've reacted really well, but now it's beginning to hit them.'

What's your attitude now to both yourself and to the children? You probably feel you want to help in some way, to entertain them perhaps – you certainly don't feel upset by them. You now realize that all the things that were going through your head about how bad and inconsiderate they were have disappeared.

The Good Habit

Develop the habit of giving *positive* frames of reference or contexts to things we see and hear. This then empowers us, helps us feel positive and keeps us energized. The good habit is to replace the bad habit of simply allowing negative frames of reference to everything that we see or hear, which tend to drive us down, tend to make us worried, frustrated and so forth.

Good mind-food can stop the sixth bad habit of allowing the wrong frame of reference to occur, and create the good habit.

Bad Habit 7: Predictably Slip Into Negative Behaviour Patterns

This habit we all have because it happens time and time again. It's typical in family situations, business situations and social situations. We set out with the best of intentions, going into a situation that's happened many times before, and, despite, supposedly, our best intentions, we come out of it having had a row, an unpleasant visit or creating bad feeling – all of which were completely predictable, based on the patterns in the past.

We blame it on the attitudes and the inconsiderateness of the other person.

The bad habit is that we do not *literally* have good intentions to avoid these things happening. At best, we have neutral intentions or, perhaps an idea of 'making an effort', but this is never enough to see us through the first crisis. It is not enough to see us through the first time the other person criticizes us unfairly, says something that's unjust or repeats one or other of the behaviour patterns that do so often happen, that lead to bad feeling.

The Good Habit.

Have good *intentions*. By intentions I mean make a deliberate plan to ensure that the visit or occasion turns out well. Specifically plan for all the things that could go wrong, and how you will change things for the better when they start going that way or how to do something different – change the usual behaviour patterns – so that the event turns out to be a success. This can apply to anything: a visit with the in-laws, Christmas with the family, a long car journey with the children, a birthday party, having people round to dinner, a business meeting, a session with the landlord, anything.

On all these occasions, you can plan ahead both activities and reactions. For example, a children's birthday party will go better when you plan a set of activities and games that will keep the children occupied and organized. Without that, chaos starts to rule and when this starts to happen, there are quickly tears and arguments. Similarly, on a long car journey, often things go wrong and you can plan your reaction for when these happen. For example, for babies you plan a series of bribes to keep them quiet. We know these techniques work, because we use them on certain occasions, but we don't use them on all occasions. We don't set out with *literally* good intentions as to what actions and reactions we can plan to make in order that the next visit or meeting is a success.

Good mind-food can stop the seventh bad habit of predictably slipping into negative behaviour and can create a good habit in its place.

Bad Habit 8: Perpetuating Bad Mind-sets

We all have mind-sets that rule our behaviour in life. Often these are limiting mind-sets of the kind:

- 'I can't do that because . . .'
- 'It's too late to make that change now.'
- 'We have to do this on Saturdays'; 'There's no time to do that'; 'It's all right for some'; 'That won't work for us.'
- 'I have to stay in my current job.'
- 'We need to do this for the sake of the children.'
- 'We'll have more time later.'
- 'There's nothing else we can do.'

Our minds are so powerful that they can find piece of evidence after piece of evidence to support the fact that that mind-set is the right one without any trouble at all. Our minds can do it in just a few seconds. If, therefore, we don't make a conscious regular habit of checking our mind-sets, we just continue with the restricted ones we have had. It's like a car that never goes in for a check-up; it's like never going to the dentist to check your teeth. In the same way, never checking your mind-sets will, sooner or later, just lead you into trouble.

The Good Habit

Regularly – say, once a week – check your mind-sets. Perhaps do this on Sundays. Think through the two or three most limiting mind-sets you have. What are the mind-sets, that, if you could change them from bad to good, might really change the quality of your life? Identify them, write them down, then change them into something more empowering. This is a good weekly habit.

Good mind-food can avoid the eighth bad habit of perpetuating bad mind-sets and can create a good habit in its place.

Bad Habit 9: Feeding the Mind the Wrong Questions

Feed your mind any question and it will come up with an answer. Ask it the question 'Why is life really such a pain?' and it will bring to the forefront of the mind all the real and imagined negative things that are around – the problems you have at work, at home, at school, with others, the problems you had in the past, the problems you expect to have in the future, the problems you have currently, the things you have to do, the worries you have and so on and so forth. It could be, however, that you are 90 per cent happy and only 10 per cent unhappy, but when asking your mind the question 'Why is life such a pain?' when your mood is really down, you get all your energies focused on the 10 per cent, look at things out of perspective and out of proportion and start feeling thoroughly miserable. Most of us, much of the day, are asking our minds the wrong question and this leads to frustration and a depressed state.

The Good Habit

Ask your mind the right questions – that open up our lives and make them even more fulfilling. For example:

- 'What are the five ways I can make today a great day for me?'
- 'What are the three things I could do tonight to make it a good evening with my family at home?'

- 'How can I enjoy myself while waiting in this queue?'
- 'How can I best use the half hour the train is delayed – who can I phone and speak to who I haven't spoken to for some time?'

Good mind-food can avoid the ninth bad habit of feeding the mind the wrong questions and create a good habit in its place.

Bad Habit 10: Focusing on Minor Things

We can, similarly, just through force of bad habit, focus our powerful minds on very small things instead of the bigger things that are important. The number of times this happens is quite staggering. Time after time, it is the smallest issues, the smallest things that put us in a bad mood, make us feel frustrated, angry or down. We dwell on them and interpret these in the worst possible fashion.

It is often only something truly traumatic, like an illness or death in the family, that helps us regain a true sense of perspective. When we're ill, especially seriously ill, we marvel at how valuable good health is. We realize how much we underappreciate the things we can do when we have it, only appreciating them when we lose it. We change our perspective. When a loved one is threatened by a serious event or even by death, we realize how much we love them and what that love means to us. Our perspective changes. In these situations, other small things are *seen* to be the small things. A bad habit however, is that this change of perspective does not last long – often within just a few days, we are back to concentrating on the small things and forgetting about the big things.

The Good Habit

Regularly train your mind to focus on the big things, those that have real value. Regularly, each week, it's a good exercise to think about the big things that you enjoy and that are going right, the big things that will make a major difference and focus your energies on them rather than dissipating your energy by focusing on a succession of small issues.

Good mind-food can avoid the tenth bad habit of focusing on minor things and can create a good habit in its place.

How Do I Put These Good Habits Into Practice?

There are many, many suggestions for good mind-food in this book. You will not be able to use all of them all of the time. In fact, if you could start by using just 10 per cent of them, 10 per cent of the time, you will have made a huge step forward in the quality of your life.

As one piece of mind-food is tried and works, you'll build to use more and more.

To help build up a menu, and a memory jogger, dedicate a small notebook or diary to writing notes in that you can carry with you easily. At the end of each chapter, take the action of writing out the short lists of mind-food in your notebook or diary for future easy reference.

Day 1 Action

1. Do the Bad Habit Quiz
How do you stand today on the above 10 bad mind-food habits? Fill in the quiz below to find out:

	Very true	True	Somewhat true	False	Very false
1 I often act closed-minded.					
2 I often accept things can't be better.					
3 My mind often 'grazes'.					
4 I often have a bad day.					
5 Remembering one thing bad helps me remember others.					
6 I often give things bad frames of reference.					
7 Visits and events often predictably slip into negative behaviour patterns.					
8 I don't regularly check my mind-sets.					
9 I often ask myself the wrong questions.					
10 I often find myself focusing on minor things.					

Now, having done the quiz, give yourself 1 mark for something that is very true, 2 for true, and so on up to 5 for very false. How do you score out of 50? If you get even half marks, already you are doing brilliantly. Most people, though, without such a course as you are now doing – will end up with only 15 or 20 out of 50. Nowhere near a good mark! Consider redoing this quiz once you've read the whole book as part of your 'weekly weighing'.

2. List the Ten Bad Mind-food Habits, Each of Which Can Be Fixed

1 Good mind-food can stop the first bad habit of acting closed-minded and can create a good habit in its place.

2 Good mind-food can stop the second bad habit of accepting there can't be a better idea and can create a good habit in its place.

3 Good mind-food can stop the third bad habit of just 'grazing' and can create a good habit in its place.

4 Good mind-food can stop the fourth bad habit of allowing yourself to have a bad day and can create a good habit in its place.

5 Good mind-food can stop the fifth bad habit of once remembering one bad thing, remembering others and can create a good habit in its place.

6 Good mind-food can stop the sixth bad habit of allowing the wrong frame of reference to occur and create a good habit in its place.

7 Good mind-food can stop the seventh bad habit of predictably slipping into negative behaviour patterns and can create a good habit in its place.

8 Good mind-food can avoid the eighth bad habit of perpetuating bad mind-sets and can create a good habit in its place.

9 Good mind-food can avoid the ninth bad habit of feeding the mind the wrong questions and create a good habit in its place.

10 Good mind-food can avoid the tenth bad habit of focusing on minor things and can create a good habit in its place.

3. Draw Pictures

Roughly draw each of the four pictures in your notebook or diary to remind yourself that there is something in them once you see it. In the same way, there is something for you in this book once you see it. There are more opportunities in life to improve the quality of your life than you currently see, but once you see how, they are easy to achieve.

4. Something to Remember

Write 'BIG IDEA–MIND FOOD' in your notebook or diary. You will get more out of life, more out of yourself and give more happiness to those around you by paying as much attention to mind-food and your mind-diet as you regularly do to body-food and body-diet.

5. Something else to Remember

Write 'THE NEW HABIT' in your notebook or diary. The new habit is to think of food for your mind as often as you consider food for your body – both what will be bad for you and what will be good for you; what you'll enjoy and what you won't. It's a good practice to notice how often we think of what to feed our bodies and at these times think of good and bad food for our *minds*, too.

The Answers to the Pictures

Figure 1 It's a cow of course! Its body is side on (with the tail out of the picture on the right) and its head turned to face you head on. Its eyes are the black spots just above the middle of the picture. Its muzzle is the dark patch close to the bottom of the picture in the centre. See it now?

Figure 2 It spells WEST. The shapes are the gaps between the letters. If you still can't see it, shade in the shapes with a pencil. See it now?

Figure 3 It is a map of the Mediterranean. The sea is the dark area and the outline of Italy is just above the centre of the picture.

Figure 4 It's a letter E. The lines form part of the outline of a capital letter E.

Day 2

Good Mind-opening Food

What Are Mind-sets?

A mind-set is the way you set your mind to look at things. The mind or brain is a very, very powerful computer. Tell it to look at things one way and it will notice, find and imagine a whole host of evidence and reasons to support the mind-set you ask it to operate on.

Success in daily life depends more on how we set our minds than on how good our minds are in the first place. This is true for individuals, for groups and it is also true for organizations. Our brain power is quite remarkable. What is just as remarkable is how often we set our brains to work in a very limiting or blinkered way. Thus, on a personal level, adopt a mind-set of 'This is going to be a bad day' and the brain will find all sorts of reasons and examples to support that point of view and cement that mood. Ask the brain 'How can we make this a great day?' and it can come up with great ideas to achieve that.

Adopt a mind-set that 'Jones is no good at dealing with people' and you'll find lots of examples in everyday life to support that particular mind-set. Adopt the alternative, 'Jones is now really good at dealing with people' and you'll find data to support that. You will set out to find Jones doing things right as opposed to setting out to catch Jones doing things wrong. You'll also get more out of Jones.

Many of our mind-sets are very strong and limiting. Consider how often the following sorts of phrases can apply:

- 'He has a closed mind.'
- 'She has a blinkered attitude towards this.'
- 'Their heads are in the sand.'
- 'They just can't see it.'
- 'They are so fixed in their attitudes.'
- 'They have a fixed mind-set on this.'
- 'He is pig-headed on this.'

Some examples of limiting mind-sets are:

- the golfer who has a mind-set 'I just can't play out of bunkers', will fluff his upcoming bunker shot
- the child who is given a mind-set 'you just can't sing' will never open her mouth to try again
- the person who has a mind-set 'they are always getting at me' will see slights and criticism where it is never intended

By contrast, some mind-sets are enabling:

- the baby who is trying to take her first step is given the mind-set 'Go on, you can do it, of course you can' and she does.
- the mind-set that says 'My spouse in many ways is getting better and better' leads to different things happening between you than the attitude that says 'My spouse is getting middle-aged'
- the mind-set 'It's easy, I've done it many times before' gives different results to the mind-set 'This time I'll mess it up'

Some of our mind-sets are quite ingrained. We almost take them as truths, even though they are simply a collection of a few data points on which the mind has drawn a conclusion. Some become so strong they can be called anything from a judgement, to a strongly held opinion, to a bias, to a prejudice.

Most mind-sets are not 100 per cent true. There is enough opportunity for an alternative mind-set. Often the alternative can be more productive, solve your problems better and help you grow and get satisfaction out of life. You just need to make a decision to change your mind-set – eat mind-food that will allow you to change.

'But', you say, 'some of my mind-sets are absolutely right. They are so true, any other mind-set is unrealistic. I'd be kidding myself.' Later there are some exercises to help you see that often there may be different ways of looking at things even when you are sure, absolutely sure, you have the right and only true way of looking at things.

Why Change Mind-sets?

Most of our mind-sets restrict the achievements of both ourselves and other individuals. Sometimes, very fixed mind-sets can be useful. They can generate rules of action that are absolutely vital and 100 per cent right. For example, when a fire breaks out, it's vital to have a bias towards action and a bias towards evacuating the building properly.

However, for every one of these rules that is helpful, there are probably 10 or 20 that are unhelpful and limiting. These can be mind-sets to do with individuals, family, problems you face in getting what you want out of life or business situations. Great energy and power can be realized by changing mind-sets from limiting ones to enabling or empowering ones.

Consider, for example, how often an individual does better when moved to a situation where they can have a fresh start. This can be a new job, a new school or a house move. Is it really that the culture or environment of the new situation is better or is it more that the individual is moving from a situation where people have fixed mind-sets about him or her, about his or her abilities and they regularly select data to reinforce these, whereas in the new situation the key aspect is that it is new and fresh? It may not necessarily be intrinsically *better*, but there is a more open mind-set about the individual and he or she can establish a new base.

Consider, similarly, how often an organization can alter as a result of a change at the top. A new broom comes in. The organization can change its mind-sets because the new boss has a new mind-set. Each individual in the organization wants to make progress, get pay rises and promotion and they realize it is politic to adopt the new mind-set of the new boss.

Without major changes, the mind-sets are those that preserve a status quo or bring fairly incremental improvement. 'It has always been like this', 'Yes, we want to do better and we are doing better' we say, but there is no trigger to make a radical change in mind-set that would bring about improvements in the performance of the individual or organization.

Imagine the power, however, if we could switch ourselves and other individuals from applying our brains in a limited or blinkered way to applying them in a mind-opening way to each situation in which we would really gain from a change. We claim that each of our mind-sets is based on history, experience, facts or on judgement. The fact is, however, that our mind-sets are mostly unnecessarily limiting.

Take, for example, a business situation in which a brand has a 10 per cent market share, which has grown over the last 3 years from 7 per cent. One collective mind-set is to celebrate the success of the brand, identify all the good things, the good work that has been done, promote the people who have worked on it and try and reapply the learnings. An alternative mind-set would be to ask the question 'Why on earth, with all the super work done over the last 3 years, are 90 per cent of customers still refusing to buy the brand and why has it taken 3 years to get that number down from 93 per cent. What is wrong with it and what can we do to make it only 50 per cent of customers who refuse to buy the brand?' Taking the second mind-set opens up far more possibilities for creative action directed at building up the business than the first mind-set does.

The same is true for success in our personal lives. Often we do not have as successful and enjoyable a life as we might have because of a series of limiting mind-sets. Imagine the things we might do if we changed some of the following:

- 'It's too late to change my job now.'
- 'We have to do this for the sake of the children.'
- 'It's too difficult to move.'
- 'We can't afford things like that.'
- 'We won't like doing that, I know it.'
- 'It's expected of us to do this, live close to them, visit him, regularly do that' and so on.
- 'We've always done this, so why change – there's nothing wrong with it.'

The power to improve our lives by choosing different mind-sets is possibly the single biggest factor in changing the potential and satisfaction in our lives.

People who can change to enabling mind-sets have fit minds; people who operate according to a series of restricting mind-sets have unfit or fixed minds.

Mind-fitness:
Fixed Minds and Flexible Minds

The terms 'fixed mind' and 'flexible mind' illustrate two extremes. No one has a fixed mind on all subjects all of the time. Nor does anyone exhibit a flexible mind on all subjects all of the time. Moreover, it is not necessarily inherently bad to have a fixed mind on many subjects, for some of the time. Often it is better to have a fixed mind until you can change it to something better than no view at all. Fixed minds help you decide on an action, cut out uncertainty and can avoid you dithering. Fixed minds help to keep things organized. Fixed minds also help people around you know where you stand and that can be helpful. Fixed minds help you to at least have something to say for yourself, have a point of view, and, in certain circumstances, that can be helpful.

This said, contrast the fixed mind with the flexible mind – overall and taken to extremes – and you will realize that there are more and more situations in which you will do better by adopting a flexible mind on an issue for a time, versus a fixed mind.

'Mind-fitness' is the ability to choose and move between the fixed mind and the flexible mind. The good mind-food of this chapter will trigger you to be able to make the moves.

Characteristics of a Fixed Mind
Taken to its extreme, the person with a fixed mind on subjects would exhibit some or all of the following:

- tends to always have a point of view
- tends to have pride in his or her opinion; tends to think it is right

- often uses slogans, stock phrases, mottoes, to guide actions on a subject
- to illustrate his or her viewpoint, tends to use the same examples over again, even if they are from a personal experience some time ago
- tends to see things as being either black or white
- ready to form a judgement quickly
- tends to ask loaded questions that support his or her point of view
- tells stories that illustrate the foolishness of others on the subject
- has fixed habits and routines
- tends to be dogmatic
- is embarrassed when shown to be wrong
- uneasy with uncertainty and woolliness; likes things settled; doesn't like non-routine things
- applies labels to situations or people; arranges instances and typifies things into a preset number of categories
- tends to distort facts to fit preconceptions on the subject
- is selective in choosing facts or instances to support preset ideas
- often an older person who thinks they are too old to change their ways
- exhibits hardening of the mind-set rather like hardening of the arteries
- has patterns of speech and patterns of thinking on the issues that are rather like rain falling on a hillside: when initially a drop falls, it forms cracks in the hillside and fixes a route and when further rain falls, it goes down into the same cracks and runs the same way and broadens them, so that, after a time, the rain can't form any new cracks but follows the existing ones and these become rivers

- doesn't think he or she can be creative; believes this is an inherent characteristic that others can show often, but he or she can show only rarely

Characteristics of a Flexible Mind

The flexible mind is more characterized by the following:

- knows when he or she has a fixed mind and chooses actively to have one
- has more creativity in thinking and an expectation that everyone can become more creative
- searches for new ideas, versus accepting the established as being the best
- looks for new points of view
- looks for new approaches
- realizes that an opinion is just a temporary point of view
- challenges the status quo
- can spot hidden assumptions
- is happy to be neutral on subjects or instances
- believes there can be more than one answer and more than one *right* answer
- questions whether facts *are* facts
- searches for better options
- comes up with better ways
- can say 'Don't know'
- is happy to *question* the group's thinking versus *following* the group's thinking
- in essence, works to avoid the restrictions, limitations and biases of the fixed mind

How to Change a Fixed Mind into a Flexible Mind

It is relatively easy. First, we need to recognize limiting mind-sets in ourselves, in individuals or an organization. Second, we need an acceptable and polite method of describing it to ourselves or others in order to achieve change. This book is designed to provide that method.

The power to change lies within each individual and with the stigma of being accused of having a closed mind, a bias or a prejudice. Even the most prejudiced people in the world, dislike being *told* that they have a prejudice. Most people would feel embarrassed if it was indicated that they had a closed mind or blinkered attitude. They would reject it and would go all out from that day to prove the exact opposite – that they don't have a blinkered or limited attitude – and so you'll achieve exactly the result you want, of more open-minded attitudes.

The trick, however, is finding a way in which to do this that is acceptable. Most people will react very defensively to being told they are prejudiced or biased in an attitude on a subject. They will think that conclusion unfair and reject it.

The following mind-opening food is designed to get you to recognize your own limiting mind-sets and to give you a common code to help get others to change their mind-sets. These pieces of mind-opening food help move us from a fixed mind to a fit mind by challenging the main mind-sets that limit our mind-fitness.

There follow five typical phrases used to support limiting mind-sets, and some mind-food to help overcome these and create more flexibility.

Mind-Set 1: 'I Don't Get Mind-sets That Lead Me to the Wrong Conclusion'

It is, however, very easy for an individual to establish a limited mind-set and get the wrong end of the stick. It's also unfortunately very easy for a group or organization to get the wrong end of the stick. This happens quite often and easily. Try the following exercises out for yourself and on a group of people.

The 'Silk' Exercise

Repeat the word 'silk' 12 times, out loud. As you call out the word 'silk', punch the air in time with it. 'Silk, silk, silk, silk, silk, silk, silk, silk, silk, silk, silk, silk.'

Now do the same thing 6 times: 'Silk, silk, silk, silk, silk, silk.'

Now 3 times: 'Silk, silk, silk.'

Now ask the question 'What do *cows* drink?' and punch the air. What answer do you think of?

The reply is probably, 'Milk.' Silk or milk? The answer is probably milk.

Now pause, relax a little and ask yourself once more 'What do cows drink?' You will come up with the right answer: 'Water.'

Try this exercise on a friend or on a group. It will work even among the brightest people, the brightest group. It will work in a group of very bright university graduates or a group of very bright managers. It will work with politicians, with academics. Indeed, it works best with anybody who *thinks* they're clever. What is happening in this exercise is that, on an individual basis, a very limiting mind-set is being set up. Each individual's mind is being directed towards the following attitude: 'I'm not going to be caught out by this guy. He wants me to say silk, without thinking; and he's going to trick me; and at some stage he's going to try to get me to say silk, when I should be saying something else. I will keep alert for what it is I should say instead of silk.'

The power of each individual mind is focused on not being caught out and on finding an *immediate* alternative solution to silk. The very mention of cows is enough to trigger an immediate quick solution to the problem the mind has been set, and it identifies milk as the alternative word to silk, even though it's completely the wrong answer to the question.

How often do you, other individuals or an organization leap to the very first answer that seems to fit one or two pieces of information and conclude rapidly, perhaps too rapidly, a solution or the best solution? How quickly do you adopt a mind-set that can lead to bias or even prejudice based on too little data?

There is a second learning point to be gained from the 'Silk' Exercise in terms of how a group or organization reacts. It is relatively easy for one individual to make a mistake and say 'milk' instead of 'water' when they are thinking that they are achieving something by saying milk instead of silk. If, however, they have around them others doing exactly the same thing, they are further reinforcing their view that they are right. Moreover, if very respected people in the organization or very bright people are also calling out 'milk', then subconsciously they know they are right and they are one of the crowd giving the same right answer.

How often does this happen to you or to your group? There may be only a few very big instances that are so big they deserve to be written about, like 'The Emperor has no clothes', but there will be a multitude of daily instances on smaller issues that are restricting you and the power of a group or organization.

The 'Toast' Exercise

This is an alternative to the 'Silk' Exercise, illustrating the same point. However, here, you can set up competition among the group members for who can be the fastest and brightest in getting the right answer. The theme of the exercise is words sounding like 'oast.' Ask a friend or a group to think fast on their feet to find a word that answers each of the following questions in turn:

- 'What do you call someone who has a guest? . . . Answer: Host.'
- 'What do you call bragging? . . . Answer: Boast.'
- 'What is a long shore by the sea? . . . Answer: Coast.'
- 'What do you do to a letter? Answer: Post.'
- 'What do you put in a toaster? Answer: Toast.'
- 'What do you do to beef? Answer: Roast.'

Normally, individuals will vie with each other to come up with the right answer first. In this situation, someone will give the answer of 'Toast' to the question 'What do you put in a toaster?' Personally, I put bread in a toaster, but in the situation where people are vying for speed, have to be thought bright in coming up with the right answer first and are preconditioned to a particular answer, it is easy to come up with 'Toast' and think it is right.

Just ask how often this happens to yourself, other individuals or an organization.

The Sign Language Exercise

Announce that this is a sign language exercise and say that you want your friend or a group to be inventive. Say 'Let's start with an easy one' and hold up the index finger and third finger of your hand to form a pair of scissors. Say:

- 'A blind man goes into a shop and wants a pair of scissors. What sort of sign would he make?' – you and the group make

the sign for scissors.
- 'He wants to buy a pen. What does he do?' – the group make a sign for writing or for a pen.
- 'He wants to buy a drink. What does he do?' – the group will make the sign of drinking out of a glass or cup.
- 'He wants to buy a dog. What does he do?' – the group will first laugh and be embarrassed because they have to imitate a dog, then some might make a growling noise, some might get down on all fours, some may even wag their 'tail' – once this is happening you say, 'Me, if I was a blind man and I wanted a dog, I'd just say, could I have a dog please?'

What has happened is that people have ignored the data and given themselves a limiting mind-set of finding a sign solution to the problem and once one member of the group does this, the rest follow suit. This is even though they've been clearly given the data that it is a blind man and not a dumb man. The limited mind-set, reinforced by others, comes up with a *really* dumb solution!

The 'Fine Night Tonight' Exercise

Ask someone to focus simply on saying the phrase 'It's a fine night tonight.' Tell them you will say three things to them and after each thing you say, all they have to do is say the phrase 'It's a fine night tonight.' Then proceed as follows:

- you say 'It's a fine night tonight.'
- the other person repeats, 'It's a fine night tonight.'
- you say 'It's a fine night *tomorrow* night.'
- the other person may say, still, 'It's a fine night tonight.'
- If so, you immediately say 'You've got it wrong, you really can't follow instructions' and they will retort, 'No I didn't, I have done exactly what you said.'

You point out the error of their ways. You said, 'It's a fine night tonight.' They said. 'It's a fine night tonight.' You said, 'It's a fine night tomorrow night.' They said, 'It's a fine night tonight.' You said, 'You've got it wrong, you can't follow instructions.' They said, 'No I didn't, I have done exactly what you said.' What they *should* have said when you questioned them following instructions was, 'It's a fine night tonight.'

The learning point of this little exercise is that when your ability is questioned, you will quickly lose track of what you should be focusing on. You adopt a mind-set of defending your own ability, which leads to a wrong answer.

The Car Crash Exercise

Imagine the following situation. A boy and his father are driving along in a car and are involved in a severe head-on car crash. They are both very badly injured and trapped in the wreckage. The ambulance arrives and manages to get the boy out first and drives him away rapidly to hospital with sirens blazing. The boy is put in a cubicle at the hospital and they summon the doctor. The doctor rushes into the cubicle, looks at the boy and says: 'Oh dear. It's Peter, my son' What is the relationship between the doctor and the boy and what has happened? Think about this for a few minutes before moving on.

People think of various solutions to this problem. For example, they think of stepfathers and stepsons. They think of situations in which the father is released from the wreckage and is flown by helicopter to the hospital and the father is actually the doctor who sees his son. Some people think of solutions that involve priests who might call someone 'my son' in a clerical way or even priests who might be called 'Father' in the first place.

The simple solution is that the doctor is the boy's *mother*. It is quite shocking and quite startling to see how many people do not find this solution easily. If it took you longer than a millisecond to get it, then the problem is your mind-set, even your prejudice.

The logic of the problem is incredibly easy: the boy has two parents, a mother and a father. If the father is still in the car wreckage, it's clear that it must be the other parent who is the doctor and that is his mother. It makes even more sense because the medical profession is one in which many females work. Therefore, if you or anybody else doesn't get the answer to this problem immediately, it *must* be due to a mind-set you have and a prejudice of associating the authoritative role of doctors with males. If you didn't find the solution immediately, don't kid yourself that you don't have limiting mind-sets.

Conclusions We Can Draw From These Exercises

Clearly mind-sets are easily formed and can lead to us giving the wrong answers. If an answer is a limiting or restrictive one, then question the mind-set that leads you to it.

Individuals and organizations quite often mix up their assessment of how clever the *argumentation* is in support of a proposal with their own views of whether that proposal is the best solution. We tend to think of cleverness as being the ability to have verbal dexterity to support a case or conclusion when *real* cleverness is the ability to decide on the best solution.

It follows that intelligent people are not always the best thinkers. They can argue their way to supporting a solution too quickly and, in many situations, they earn too much respect from others because of their cleverness in this area. However, this very skill stops them short of coming up with the best solution.

A better thinker or problem-solver will not accept the first solution. They can find argumentation to support it, but they will ask mind-opening questions and develop alternative solutions. They will use an objective method of evaluating the alternatives, for example looking at the plusses and minuses of each alternative solution.

This approach is likely to achieve the most effective and far-reaching solution to any problem. However, this skill is not always recognized. We tend to have a bias for action. We like to close down on certainty. This is like the doctor and the remedy. If we go to the doctor with a pain in our stomach, we value the doctor saying quite confidently what it is, giving us a few pills and sending us away with the prospect of the pain going away. By contrast, we would find it unsettling if the doctor told us the 13 things that could be wrong with us and then went through a painstaking analysis, eliminating each possibility in turn, leaving us with just a probability, but not a certainty, and more tests to be done, even though this is likely to be the more effective method in the long run.

In solving your problems, then, make sure that you are not visiting the doctor for an instant remedy when you should be doing something else.

Mind-sets are powerful. The most vivid example is war. What else but the most powerful mind-set could cause you or I to join an army and go to war? Why would we do something where the very, very best we could hope for would be to come home alive as we are now, with the same family, same number of limbs, same health . . . and high odds we would not even do that? It's easy, though, to get a nation to go to war – you just need to engender three mind-sets:

- the nation is being attacked or will be attacked
- anyone who doesn't join the army to fight is not a patriot, is a traitor to their country, friends, society and family
- when in the army, form groups of a dozen or so and make each individual in them have the mind-set of not letting down

their buddies in the group

With these mind-sets you or I will willingly do things that will get us killed.

Essentially then, we can conclude the following:

- it's easy to get into a mind-set that limits your mind-fitness and can lead you to the wrong conclusions
- beware group mind-sets that are limiting you in what you want to achieve – the power of group dynamics can make people follow like sheep, even to war
- It's poor mind-fitness to use your intelligence simply to support the reasons you give as to why your answer or opinion is the right or best one; instead, use it to seek a better one

What Action Can We Take?
Feed the mind the food of the results of:

- the 'silk' exercise
- the 'toast' exercise
- the 'sign language' exercise
- the 'fine night tonight' exercise
- the 'car crash' exercise

to realize when you have a limiting fixed mind-set. Give this mind-food to others too. It will help them move on to a mind-set that will be more helpful.

Mind-set 2: 'This is Right, That is Wrong'
Once a person has an answer to a problem, it's difficult to see that there's any other answer. His or her mind is made up. Here are some illustrations of this phenomenon.

What is This a Picture of?

Figure 5

The answer given to this question depends heavily on one's instant reaction to it. Did you see an old lady or a young lady? If you saw it one way, it will be difficult to see it any other way. It can also depend on preconditioning. Show Figure 11 (see page 57) to one person first. Show Figure 27 (see page 66) to another person first, Then show each the above picture. What answer do they give? One will have the mind-set that it is a young lady and will be unlikely to see it any other way. The other will have the mind-set that it is an old lady and will be unlikely to see it as a young lady. Show each the other picture and the mind can change its mind-set. The mind has been 'opened.'

What is This a Picture of?

Figure 6

Show one person the following sequence of words before showing them this picture:

America, Wild West, buffalo, pony

Show another person the following sequence of words before showing them the picture:

Person, house, Arctic, ice

Because of the preconditioning, one person will see this picture as an Indian, the other will see it as an Eskimo going into an igloo.

What is This a Picture of?

Figure 7

Show one person the following sequence of numbers before showing them this picture:

12, 14

Show another person the following sequence of letters before showing them the picture:

A, C

It is clear what the two answers will be.

Conclusions We Can Draw From These Exercises
We can conclude the following:

- good mind-fitness is recognizing that there is more than one way of looking at things; someone else can be equally right when something is looked at from their point of view.
- good mind-fitness is recognizing that how you view things and the answers you come up with will be heavily biased by what you've experienced so others with different experiences will see things differently
- always consider both sides of the case

What Action Can We Take?
Feed the mind the food of the results of the:

- old lady/young lady picture
- Eskimo/Indian picture
- 13/B picture

to help yourself see different points of view that may be more helpful. Offer the mind-food to others too to help them open their minds to *your* point of view.

Mind-set 3: 'There's Nothing in That'
Often people will use the phrase 'there's nothing in that.' Here are some examples to illustrate the fact that sometimes there can be more in an idea than is seen at first glance. The answers to each of these puzzles are given at the end of this chapter.

Do These Lines Represent Anything?

Figure 8

Is There Anything in This Picture?

Figure 9

Does This Represent Anything?

Figure 10

Conclusions We Can Draw From These Exercises

In each of these pictures (like those you saw in Day 1) at first glance, there doesn't appear to be much. If one's mind-set is that there is nothing to see, there will be nothing to see. However, by virtue of being an exercise in this book, your mind-set is the opposite to this. As you looked through these pictures, your mind-set was 'there is something in these pictures to see' and, as a result, you have found something.

The fit mind will not reject an idea or a suggestion just because, initially, it 'can't see anything in it.' Most people do not deliberately make suggestions that are completely stupid;

they make suggestions that make sense to them. The unfit mind rejects them when it can't immediately see the sense; the fit mind seeks to see what's in it.

What Action Can We Take?
Feed your mind the food of the results of the exercises:

- letter E picture
- Jesus Christ picture
- Dalmatian picture
- cow picture
- word WEST picture
- Mediterranean map picture

to help yourself not reject suggestions out of hand, but to 'see what's in them.' Feed the food to others too to help them be open to *your* suggestions.

Figure 11

Mind-set 4: It's Clear From the Facts

Mind-sets can develop from what you *think* you know, but that can be misleading. How do you *know* what you think you know? Very little of it comes from direct personal experience. Depending on how much 'knowledge' you profess, it's likely that no more than 10 or 20 per cent comes from direct personal experience. About 50 per cent may come from what other people have told you and 20 per cent or so from assumptions you've drawn and inferences you've made. The balance, of course, can be different from person to person and from subject to subject, but it's clear that what you believe to be facts are mostly reliant on the reports of others and assumptions or inferences you yourself have made. Moreover – even on the 10 or 20 per cent you *personally* observe – how much of that is right?

Look at This Picture
How many right angles are there in this picture?

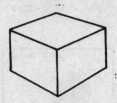

Figure 12

Look at This Picture
Are there no triangles here, 2, 6, or 8?

Figure 13

Look at These Pictures
Are these perfect squares?

Figure 14

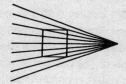

Figure 15

Look at This Picture
Is the small circle a perfect one?

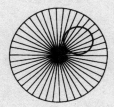

Figure 16

Look at This Picture
Are the dark lines straight?

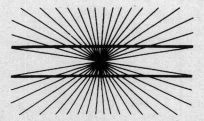

Figure 17

Conclusions We Can Draw From These Exercises

The answers to the above puzzles are of course that there are no right angles, no triangles, no imperfect squares, no imperfect circles and no unstraight lines. It just seems that there are. The brain actually adds details that aren't there in order to form a pattern it's seen before or sometimes just adds because of the context. If one can be so mistaken by just a simple visual representation, how easy is it to be mistaken about something as complex as a business problem or a person's performance?

Similarly, is this picture rows of dots or columns of dots?

. . . .
. . . .
. . . .
. . . .

Figure 18

Is this picture rows of dots or columns of dots?

. . . .
. . . .
. . . .
. . . .

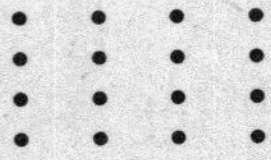

Figure 19

Is this picture rows of dots or columns of dots?

. . . .
. . . .
. . . .
. . . .

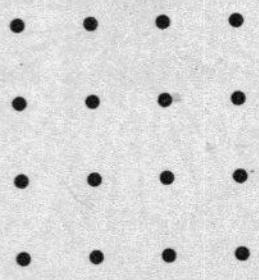

Figure 20

The one answer is that none of these pictures are rows of dots or columns of dots – they are all simply a matrix of dots. How we decide to conclude they are lines or rows is purely subjective, normally based on where the dots are closer to each other. If they happen to be closer next to each other in a row, the brain interprets them as rows; if they happen to be closer to each other in a column, we call then columns; if they happen to be coloured alternately in rows, we call them rows; if they happen to be coloured alternately in columns, we call them columns. There is, however, no factual basis for this – it's just a casual link we make.

Next time you are in a business situation or considering a person's potential of performance, identify any casual links that you think have been made inappropriately, particularly if they lead to limiting mind-sets.

What famous phrase is here?

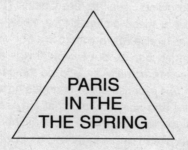

Figure 21

Clearly, it is 'Paris in the spring.' The brain can simply choose to omit details as well as adding them in order to get things to conform to a previous pattern. In this instance, it simply deletes the second 'the'.

Think of a footstep. Imagine a footstep. What did you think of?

If you imagined yourself in a room late at night, alone in bed and imagined a footstep outside the door, you'll probably feel fear and act that way.

If, however, you imagined yourself at home, anxiously awaiting the return of your child who has been out later than usual and is overdue getting home and you imagine a footstep outside the door, you'll feel joy and act that way.

By contrast, if you are walking to work in the middle of the rush hour and you hear a footstep, it means nothing. It is just one of thousands being made all round you and the effect is neutral.

Similarly, imagine the lights of a car a few cars behind you on the motorway, approaching quickly. If you are speeding, do you mistakenly interpret that car as a police car?

The point is that we easily give extra meaning to facts, simply by the frame of reference we happen to put them in.

As a further exercise, to check how obvious things *seem*, consider the following visual representations. Normally, when someone looks at these pictures, they 'know' that they are actually illusions or else why put them in a book? The mind-set is 'A *looks* bigger than B, but I *know* this is an exercise in illusion, so they are *actually* likely to be the same length.'

However, in *this* exercise some changes have been made. Thus some *are* and some *aren't* what they seem. Thus it's impossible to use the logic that 'A looks as though it's bigger than B, but because I'm being tricked as to which is bigger, it probably means that B is bigger'.

Now, for each set of pictures, decide whether A is bigger than B or whether both are the same size.

Which is bigger, the line in A, the glasses, or the line in B, the dumbell?

GLASSES

DUMBELL

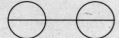

Figure 22

Which line here is longer?

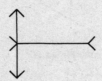

Figure 23

Which is longer - line AB or BC?

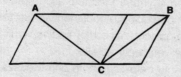

Figure 24

Which inner circle is larger?

Figure 25

Which is bigger – line A or B?

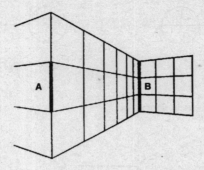

Figure 26

The answers are at the end of this chapter. If it is difficult enough to decide on a simple issue as to whether A is bigger than B, and get the right answer, think how difficult it is for something more complicated like a business situation or a person. Therefore, distrust your immediate assumption that 'it is clear from the facts', particularly if that clarity is just feeding a limiting mind-set or a preconceived prejudice, which may not be giving you the very best answer.

Does familiarity help or not? In some cases, being familiar with a problem can help when interpreting the data; in other cases it doesn't help in deciding whether it's obvious or not. Take the following examples:

You are shown four cards and on the side of the cards you see are the letters and numbers A, F, 3, 2. You are asked to solve the problem of which cards you need to turn up to check whether the following statement is true or untrue: 'Cards with a vowel on one side have an even number on the other side.' What is the answer? Consider the problem now, and jot some notes here.

Most people will answer that you need to turn over the A. Others may also add that you need to turn over the 2.

In fact, you need to turn over the A and the 3. If there is an odd number on the other side of the A, the statement is clearly untrue. If there is a vowel on the other side of the 3, the statement is clearly untrue. If neither of these occurs, the data would support that the statement is true.

The *unfamiliarity* of the *terms* of this problem stops you seeing how 'obvious' the answer is.

By contrast, if you pose the same problem of logic in *familiar terms*, the answer is easy. If the problem is posed as cards showing Beer, Lemonade, 16 and 20, and you are asked to check the familiar problem of making sure that nobody under 18 is drinking alcohol, you would quickly recognize that you need to check the 16 year-old and the person drinking beer.

Here, the familiarity of the problem and the situation helps in the correct solution of exactly the same logical problem that you stumble over when it is unfamiliar.

By contrast, sometimes familiarity breeds contempt. We assume we know the logic when we don't. For example, if a man says to his son, 'I will give you £5 if you mow the lawn', the familiarity of the situation will cause us to be misled on the logic. We will assume that if he *doesn't* mow the lawn, he will *not* get the £5. However, the logic is not necessarily there. He will not necessarily not get the £5 if he doesn't mow the lawn; nor is mowing the lawn the *only* way he will get £5. For example, if he said he couldn't mow the lawn, we might offer him an alternative task to receive this sum, say, to wash the car.

We should learn to be cautious in familiar surroundings as to whether familiarity is breeding contempt. If the mind-set for the solution is a limiting one, question whether overfamiliarity with a situation is causing this.

In essence, the conclusions we can draw from this are:

- the fit mind recognizes that much of what it thinks it knows, it doesn't – most of what it knows relies on what it's been told by other people – so good mind-fitness is being wary of 'facts' given by people who have a vested interest in the outcome
- the fit mind recognizes that it can be mistaken, even in what it experiences directly
- good mind-fitness is recognizing that the 'facts that make it clear' can often be safely questioned, if the answer they suggest is inadequate for what you need
- familiarity with the situation may help, but may also hinder

What Action Can We Take?
Feed your mind the mind-food of the results of the exercises:

- right angles, triangles, squares, circles and lines pictures
- lines or rows of dots pictures
- 'Paris in the spring' picture
- footstep and police car visualizations
- A bigger than B diagrams
- A, F, 3, 2 card question

to realize that sometimes the facts you think are clear aren't. Do this whenever the facts limit you. Offer the mind-food to others whenever they are 'stuck' on a particular course because 'the facts are clear'.

Figure 27

Mind-set 5: 'I Can Change my Mind-set, It's Changing Other People's That's Impossible.'

Here is a clear strategy that *will* help change others' mind-sets: *use this book*.

The examples shown in this chapter have been designed to help you, in a friendly way, not only change *your* mind-sets but change those of *others*.

Remember, even the worst bigot on an issue, will be embarrassed to be found to be one and will work actively to show that they are not. They will become flexible and tolerant, just to prove to you that they are not narrow-minded on the issue.

The problem has been how to broach the subject in a way that isn't confrontational. Now you can use samples of the drawings, exercises and anecdotes of this chapter to broach the subject in a light-hearted and non-threatening way.

The Conclusion We Can Draw From This Chapter
It is that:

- the fit mind recognizes that you can not only change your own mind-sets for the better, you can change others too.

What Action Can We Take?
Use some of the mind-food of this chapter tomorrow on something or someone you want to influence. Have fun!

The answers to the pictures
Figure 8 It is a letter E.
Figure 9 It is a picture of Jesus Christ. He is facing you head-on, with his body turned slightly to the right, wearing a sort of cloak. You see him from the chest up. His eyes are the two black spots near the top of the picture in the middle; he has a beard, and the bottom of the beard is about dead-centre of the picture; he has long dark hair coming down to his shoulder just to the left of the bottom of the beard. See it now?

Figure 10 This is a dalmatian.

The answers to whether A or B is bigger
The glasses are actually larger than the dumbell. In all the other exercises the figures are the same size.

Day 3

Mind-food For Creative Thinking

What is Creative Thinking?

You have now learned some good mind-food for opening up your mind and making it fitter and opening up the minds of others. There is still more you can do to help release the best creative thinking you are capable of, which will help you achieve what you want and be as happy and successful as you can be.

Many people are frightened of the words 'creative thinking'. They think they apply to somebody else, not to them. Many have an attitude to this that is almost a mind-set – 'I'm not a creative person' or 'Creativity doesn't apply to me, it applies to other people, like artists, singers and dancers.'

Creativity is simply the formation of new ideas. It is expressing things in a new way. No more and no less than that. The reasons we associate artists, musicians and sculptors with creativity are, first that there is a physical, notable output to their creativity and second, that these people probably have the sort of fit minds that are prepared to try things, prepared to experiment, not afraid to make a mistake. That is probably how they got into art or sculpture in the first place. By contrast, many other people are not prepared to 'let themselves go' early on in life and paint, sing and take the risk of being humiliated when people hear or see their product.

For example, consider for a moment whether the next generation will or will not be, on average, better singers than the last generation. One reason for why they may be is the ever-present Karaoke game and its popularity. It encourages people to open their mouths and try singing, who, previously, would have shied away from it. There is now a mind-set that it's good to try to sing, whereas previously a poor singer would have been discouraged early. As a result of this, on average, we should have better singers.

In the same way, we can encourage more and more people to improve the fitness of their minds and show some creative thinking.

Barriers to Creative Thinking

Your brain is quite capable of producing the new ideas that we call creative thinking. The new ideas we want to focus on are those that will help us achieve more and get more out of our lives. Changing one's mind-set is the first prerequisite to this process, but there can still be barriers that restrict our thinking. Imagine these as small blockages in our brain, that restrict the power of our thinking from gaining access to 80 or 90 per cent of the world's smallest, yet, at the same time, most powerful super-computer.

Following are some pieces of mind-food to help remove a few barriers that may stay in the way of us getting the very best ideas we can for solving the problems we face, whether they be personal, business or of the kind that stop us getting the very best out of our lives.

Barrier 1: The Answer is Clear

The Squares Exercise

How many squares are there in this picture?

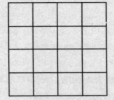

Figure 28

One answer is clearly 16 and that is a right answer. Is it the *only* right answer, though, or the *best* right answer? It is if you assume that a square is simply the *smallest* square shown.

Look again and there are bigger squares. The big surrounding square is itself a square. Each of the four quarters of the big square is a square. There are three by three squares. Counting them all, there are, in fact, 16 small squares; 9 squares 2 by 2; 4 squares 3 by 3; and one square 4 by 4. In total 30 squares.

There is more than one right answer, but if you are looking for the answer of the *most* number of squares, any answer under 30 is wrong.

The Lines and Dots Exercise

What is the minimum number of straight lines you need to join up these nine dots, if you are not allowed to take your pen off the paper and can only move in straight lines?

Figure 29

Think about this problem now, before you turn the page. Try out different ways in the space below.

A common answer is five.

Figure 30

Is there a better answer? Indeed there is, you can do it in four if you try harder. The way to do it is as follows:

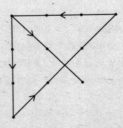

Figure 31

To think of this solution, you need to free your mind of the self-imposed restriction of only drawing lines within the boundaries of the nine dots. You may have felt that the words above and below the dots were a sort of barrier and that the lines had to be drawn without crossing over the text.

This is clearly a good answer – some of you may even have seen this answer before – but is this the *minimum* number of lines you can do it in?

No. You can do it in *three* if you simply, instead of using a pen with narrow nib, elect to choose as your implement a very wide-nibbed marker pen. No one told you what width pen to use – you imposed your own barrier.

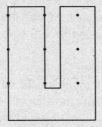

Figure 32

Is that it? No, you can do it in *one*.

Simply, fold the paper along the gaps midway between the lines of dots and concertina the paper up, so that the figure becomes, effectively, one line of three, each of three dots, and simply join them up with a pencil, pen or anything. You probably felt the barrier of needing to keep the paper flat.

There is often more than one right answer and your *first* right answer is often not necessarily your *best*. Remove self-imposed barriers and you can find better and better answers.

The Numbers Exercise

How do you turn 'VI' into seven by adding one line?

The answer is to add a line and make 'VII', the Roman numeral for seven.

How do you turn 'IX' into six by adding one single line?

Think about this before going to the next page. Use the space below to try out different ideas.

One answer is to add in the single line 'S' before the 'IX' and make 'SIX'. You need good mind-fitness to find this solution as you need to dissociate yourself from the pattern of solving the previous problem (making VI into seven) in solving the new one.

Is that the right answer? Is there another? Yes. You could draw a horizontal line through the 'IX' halfway up, then turn the figure upside down and the top will represent the Roman numeral VI for six. You don't *have* to dissociate to get a right answer.

The Letters Exercise

Cross out six letters from the following sequence so that the remaining letters, without altering their sequence, spell a well-known word:

B S I A N X L A E T N T A E R S

Try it now for five or ten minutes before moving on.

It looks pretty impossible doesn't it?

The answer is 'BANANA'. You get it by removing the letters 'S I X L E T T E R S' from the sequence. It requires good mind-fitness, and a mind-set to consider looking at the problem in different ways.

This is clearly the right answer – isn't it?

An alternative approach would be to choose six letters and remove them *each time* they appear in the sequence. By choosing 'XIANBS' and removing them, you end up with the word LETTER.

Again the barrier is thinking that the first right answer is the best one. Keep looking for more right answers, then choose the best from among *them*.

Subsidiary Barrier: Group-think

Ask a group to tackle the above problems and it's almost a certainty that the group will never – no matter how bright the individuals – come up with the second or third answers. The reason is the barrier of 'group-think.'

Typically, a group spends only a limited time in a meeting thinking of new ideas to solve a problem. Often one or two of the members can push the meeting in a particular direction. Once a solution starts being formed, a consensus starts being built and the pressures of the group push the other members into accepting it. Prolonged discussion or thinking is received, then, with impatience. The group will look for a second or third answer and then choose between them only rarely. Try the previous examples of exercises with a group to see group-think in action.

Now try this. Imagine a row of three empty glasses, next to three full glasses. By touching and moving just *one* glass, how could you rearrange things so that no empty glass is next to an empty glass and no full glass next to a full glass?

Take a few minutes now to think about it.

A solution is to take the middle full glass, pour its contents into the middle empty glass, then return it to its place.

It requires mind-fitness – being prepared to look at things a different way and having the mind-set of looking for different sorts of solutions – to come up with this idea.

Next one. How many people do you need to have in a hall for there to be an almost certain chance that you have two people with the same birthday in a group? What would you judge the answer to be – 365, 183, somewhere in between? Could it really be fewer than 183?

Think about it for a few minutes before moving on. Jot your answers down here.

The answer, by law of probability is 70 and you need only 29 people to have a 50:50 chance of finding 2 with the same birthday. It isn't 'obvious'. In fact, after reading the answer, many people will still disbelieve it, although statistically it is true.

Here, the true answer is in conflict with your current perspective, which in fact has been based on some false assumptions.

Try the following. Would you recognize your mother?

Of course you would. The clear answer is 'yes'. Would you pick her out from a group of 50 women of a similar age and background? Of course you could. Easily? Of course you could, provided that the faces were close up and visible. So, we'll make it easy. The faces will be passport photos in rows and columns. Could you pick out your mother from among 50 passport photos provided hers is a good likeness? Of course you could. The answer is obviously 'yes'.

However, you couldn't if the columns and rows of passport photos were shown to you upside down. The mind is absolutely brilliant at facial recognition: you can pick out friends and relations from among the crowds, from among a million people, but *only* if you see their face the right way up. See their faces upside down and you cannot recognize your own mother. Test this out for yourself.

Here the answer is clear, but only if it is in an assumed context.

What Conclusions Can We Draw From These Exercises?
- the fit mind recognizes that the first answer it finds is often not a good one, no matter how well it can support it; it recognizes that there is often more than one right answer and seeks new ideas that lead to better answers
- the fit mind removes self-imposed boundaries in finding new ideas for answers
- good mind-fitness also means questioning the context that is assumed for any answer it seeks and puts things in new contexts to find better answers
- good mind-fitness recognizes that group-think dynamics, often, are limiting in finding the best answer

What Action Can We Take?
Feed your mind the food of the results of the:

- the squares exercise
- the lines and dots exercise
- the numbers exercise
- the letters exercise
- the glasses exercise

- the birthday exercise
- the recognizing your mother exercise

to continue to search for new ideas for better answers, particularly when the first one is inadequate for your purposes. Feed the food to others too who are 'stuck' on a particular answer.

Barrier 2: The Pattern is Clear

The Anagram Solutions Exercise

See how quickly you can solve the following series of anagrams, in order. When you solve the first one, shout out the answer and then move to the second and so on:

1 REZAB
2 NOLI
3 KOMYEN
4 RETGI
5 LECMA
6 YNOP
7 HICAR

Take a few minutes to do this.

Note how quickly you find the solutions. The first one is clearly zebra, the second lion, the third monkey, the fourth tiger, the fifth camel and the sixth pony. How often people will stumble with number 7. All previous solutions have been animals and number 7 looks as though it should be some form of rare animal with letters like that, but it's difficult to bring it to mind. In fact, the solution is chair. It has nothing to do with animals, but it's easy for an individual or a group to get into a mind-set that all the solutions will be an animal simply because the first six have been.

The Alphabet Exercise

Some patterns are absolutely essential to help us. For example, you know the pattern of the alphabet. You also know the necessary pattern for counting. You probably also know how to count backwards in order, because you've needed the pattern at some stage: 10, 9, 8, 7, 6, etc. Could you, however, recite the alphabet, backwards, starting from Z? Try it now. This pattern is not very useful, so it is not used and so you probably have difficulty doing it.

The Days in the Month Exercise

Similarly, how many days are there in October? You *may* know off-hand, but you are more likely to use a learned pattern in the form of a verse – in order to get to the right answer. In fact, the only way for most people to get the answer right is to recite internally 'Thirty days has September, April, June and November. All the rest have 31, except February which has 28 days clear, and 29 each leap year.' It is really almost incredible that the only way we know how many days there are in any one of our months is by repeating this pattern.

This pattern of course, relies for its effectiveness on the English language as this forms the rhymes that make it memorable. What patterns are used to find the days in a month by people who speak other languages? You will find a common pattern is to use the knuckles on the hand. The way to do this is to close the fist and view each knuckle as being a month that has 31 days; and the valley of flesh between the knuckles as being a month with fewer than 31 days. So, starting at one end of the fist on the knuckles, you count January, which is on a peak (31); February, which is in a valley (28); March, a peak (31), April, a valley (30); May, a peak (31); June, a valley (30); July, a peak (31); double-tap the end knuckle and return to get August, a peak (31); September, a valley (30); October, a peak (31); November, a valley (30); and December a peak (31).

The I before E Exercise

How do you know whether a word is spelled 'EI' or 'IE'? You probably recite the following rhyme to yourself: 'I before E except after C.' This is a very useful pattern, but it is also limiting. How about 'neighbour' which doesn't obey the rule, and we know that there are several others that don't obey the rule either.

You might have heard this pattern being extended – 'I before E, except after C and before G' – to take account of words like 'neighbour'. However, even this isn't foolproof. It doesn't take account of words like 'siege'.

People have therefore tried to extend this pattern to say 'I before E, except after C and before a *soft* G.' This also takes into account the spelling of words like 'reign'. However, this pattern isn't always right either because it doesn't take account of words like 'beige'.

The full pattern needed to cover *all* instances in the English language is:

I before E
Except after C
Or when sounded like A
As in 'neighbour' or 'weight'
Or when sounded like IGHT
As in 'height' or 'sleight'.

The Letter Pattern Exercise

Finally, what is this a pattern of?

QWERTYUIOP

This pattern is easily recognizable to anybody who has used a typewriter or computer keyboard. It's known as the QWERTY pattern. Why is it arranged this way on a typewriter? The logical answer would be that it has been designed in order for the typist to type with the maximum of speed and efficiency. It clearly makes sense not to arrange the letters in order of the alphabet, but instead to arrange them in a pattern that meets the needs of how frequently a letter is needed to be typed and the ease of typing it with each of the fingers. The fact that the Q, an infrequent letter, is to the far left to be typed by the left little finger, reinforces this. You probably think, therefore, that this is the 'best' configuration one could have for a keyboard for efficient typing.

In fact, this pattern is based on exactly the *opposite* thinking. It was designed over 100 years ago by manufacturers of typewriters who found that the keys were sticking together too often if the operator typed too fast. They therefore designed a pattern that would *slow down* the operator and thereby avoid the keys sticking. It has the very frequent letters, I and O, in positions to be typed by the less strong fingers. This is how the QWERTY pattern came about.

Of course, since then, technology has advanced enormously and there is no chance of the keys sticking together, but the whole world is stuck with a pattern that was specifically designed to *decrease* speed rather than *increase* it.

Conclusion

Patterns can be useful, but patterns can also be limiting. Be ready to remove or change patterns when they're a barrier to the production of new ideas.

Action

Feed your mind the food of the results of:

- The Anagram Solutions Exercise
- The Alphabet Exercise
- The Days in the Month Exercise
- The I Before E Exercise
- The Letter Pattern Exercise

to help seek new ideas when patterns may be misleading or limiting you.

Barrier 3: 'Impossible, It Can't Be Done'

Anything can be done, once you know how. Ask the mind opening question 'How can it be done?', not the mind-closing question 'Can it be done?'. Consider the following:

The Remembering Exercise Part One

Could you remember the following 10 objects and say which object corresponds with which number, even when the numbers are asked out of order?

1 Helicopter
2 Cigar
3 Guitar
4 Newspaper
5 Radio
6 Paint
7 Briefcase
8 Lawn
9 Financial Times
10 Priest

The answer to this is probably, 'no'.

Ask the question 'How could this be done?' and the answer is as follows. The way to do this is to visually associate pictures conjured up by each number and item. Link one picture to another in an absurd way in your brain and visualize it for an instant. For example, think of an elephant sitting on your wife's head. The next time you see your wife's head, you'll think of an elephant. This is the principle of visual 'association'.

You need to associate each of these objects with one of the numbers from 1 to 10. To do this, you must make the numbers 1 to 10 mean something to you in visual terms. There's a simple rhyme to do this: 1-bun; 2-shoe; 3-three; 4-door; 5-jive; 6-sticks; 7-heaven; 8-gate; 9-wine; 10-pen. Repeat this rhyme for yourself and remember it.

Next, the first object needs to be linked with a bun. Link a helicopter with a bun. Imagine a bun and imagine the helicopter coming down to land on top of the bun. The bun is giant, the helicopter is small. The helicopter sinks into the bun. Now visualize it, then move on.

You continue in this way down the list. The second number is 2-shoe and the second object is 'cigar'. Imagine the shoe smoking the cigar. Put the cigar in the front of the shoe and imagine the cigar plugging into it, the end of the cigar is lit and smoke is coming from it.

Now move on to the number 3-tree and the third object, 'guitar'. Imagine a guitar stuck in a tree. The guitar is absolutely huge, it's almost as big as the tree itself.

Then move on to the fourth number 4-door and the fourth object, 'newspaper'. Imagine a door made out of a full front page of a newspaper. As you go to open the door, you actually push back a newspaper. The door is very flimsy.

Then move on to 5-jive. The fifth object is 'radio'. Remember, the secret is not to make the visual link logical. Make it illogical and exaggerated. Make it full of movement. Imagine people jiving and there is a radio in the middle of the floor, but it's not playing music, it's blaring out the news headlines. Imagine it and stop.

Move on to 6-sticks. The sixth object is 'paint'. Imagine the sticks in a fire, waiting to be lit, and it can't be lit because a can of paint is poured all over it.

Move on to 7-heaven and the seventh object, 'briefcase'. Imagine heaven in the sky and a big briefcase falling down and hitting you on the head.

Move on to 8-gate. The eighth object is a lawn. Imagine a gate and you're about to open it, but you actually open a gate made out of lawn. It's not made of wood or iron, it's made of pure grass or lawn. Imagine it and move on to the next.

Next is 9-wine. The object is the *Financial Times*. The *Financial Times* is pink. Imagine an open bottle of wine and wrapped into the top of it, instead of a cork, there is a tightly wrapped *Financial Times*. You can't pour the wine, because the *Financial Times* is in the way.

Then move on to 10-pen. The object is a priest. Imagine a pen that you use, and instead of writing on paper, you are writing on a priest's white collar.

Now it's easy to remember those objects. What is number 5? The link word for 5 is jive. Remember the jive and instead of music it was the news coming from a *radio*.

What is number 3? The link word for 3 is tree. Imagine the tree and see again the guitar in the tree.

What is the object for 7? The link word is heaven. Remember heaven and remember the big briefcase coming down and hitting you on the head. And so on.

It's not impossible, it's easy – once you know how to do it.

The Remembering Exercise Part Two

Do you think you could remember 52 playing cards in any order once you have seen them once? The probable answer to this is no.

Ask the question, 'How could I remember 52 playing cards in any order once I have seen them once' and the answer is as follows.

As with the first question, you need to get the numbers 1 to 52 and each card to mean something to you in visual terms. Once a number means something to you in visual terms, you simply link that object with the object for the card, then for any number you will remember the card.

For example, if the link for number 32 is 'moon' and the card you remembered is 4 of hearts, and that means 'hare', you can imagine a big hare jumping right over the moon in the sky. When you think of 'moon' you'll remember 'hare'.

You get the numbers to mean something to you by means of a phonetic alphabet. There are only 10 sounds in the phonetic alphabet. Link each sound with a number as follows: 1=t; 2=n; 3=m; 4=r; 5=l; 6=sh; 7=ck or ch; 8=f; 9=p or b; 0=s. When you need an object to correspond with a number, simply take the sound for the number and link them with a vowel. So 32 is an 'm' followed by an 'n' or a 'moon'. All you need to remember is the 10 sounds, corresponding to each number and then any number can mean an object to you, that you can decipher. For example, '67' is a 'shack'. Write out now in the space below your own objects for the numbers 1 to 52.

Using the phonetic alphabet you now need each *card* to mean something to you in object terms. The object will begin with the letter of the suitable card, so each club begins with a C, each heart with an H, each spade with an S and each diamond with a D. Then simply use the phonetic sound for the number. For example a 7 of diamonds is a 'd' followed by a 'ck', producing 'deck'. If the 7 of diamonds came up as number 32, associate the deck of a ship breaking through the moon and splitting it in half. When it comes to number 32, remember 3 and 2 'moon', picturing the moon will allow you to remember 'deck', deciphering deck will tell you the card is the 7 of diamonds. The 32nd card is the 7 of diamonds.

A few small alterations need to be made for the 'picture' cards. For the jacks simply remember the suit. So the jack of clubs is a 'club'; the jack of spades is a 'spade'; the jack of diamonds is a 'diamond'; and the jack of hearts is a 'heart'. For the queens, think of an object that sounds like queen, that starts with the letter of the suit. So the queen of clubs is 'cream'; the queen of spades is 'stream'; the queen of diamonds is 'dream' and for the queen of hearts simply use 'queen'.

For the kings do the same thing. The king of clubs is 'king', the king of hearts is 'hinge', the king of spades is 'sing' and the king of diamonds is 'dinge'.

There you are. Here is a simple system that, with a little work, will help you remember 52 playing cards in any order when you have seen them once. There is no such thing as 'it can't be done', the only question is 'How can it be done?'

The Bishop and the Thief

Could you do the following?

Photocopy this page of the book and trim it to the same size. Fold it just three times, then tell the following story.

A bishop and a thief died at exactly the same time. I want you to imagine them on the road leading to either heaven or hell. The bishop is ahead, the thief runs to catch up. They start talking. The thief starts talking to the bishop and says to him, 'I'm really worried. I've been a thief all my life, and I'm certain to go to hell.' The bishop shows sympathy towards him and says that he is sorry. He has been a good bishop all his life and he really hopes to go to heaven. Indeed, he has in his hand his mitre and this he thinks is his pass into heaven. The shape is like this.

Figure 33

The thief is quite crafty and says to the bishop, 'Surely bishop, you need to show charity. You've been a bishop all your life. That is good enough to get into heaven. You also have a pass. Shouldn't you really give a poor person like me your pass?'

The bishop thinks about this for some time and decides that the thief has a point. He doesn't give him *all* his pass however; he decides to give him a piece. He tears off one third as shown overleaf, holding the mitre by the tip.

Figure 34

The thief thanks him and they continue to walk up the road. The thief, though, hasn't given up yet and he says to the bishop, 'Bishop, I'm really only doing you a favour, but I must point out that you have kept the bigger half. Surely that will look bad to St Peter when you finally have to go to heaven? That will look a little selfish. Why don't you give me half of what is left and then at least you'll still have a part, but I will have the bigger part.'

The bishop thinks about this and once again, he decides that the thief is right and he tears off half of what is left (as shown below) and gives it to the thief.

Figure 35

At this point, the thief decides that this is about as much as he will get and he decides to leave the bishop and go on ahead of him.

He arrives at heaven's gates, sees St Peter, goes up to him and says, 'Let me in, let me in, here I am. I have got two-thirds of a pass into heaven.'

St Peter says, 'That's very good, but why don't we wait a minute. Let me look at the pieces of paper you have, and sort them out.' St Peter takes the bits of paper, sorts them out and they form the pattern shown below.

Figure 36

'I'm afraid', he says, 'you're going to the other place.'

The thief is furious. He crumples up the pass, moves away back down to the road towards the other place, and he meets the bishop coming along. 'Bad luck', he says to the bishop, 'you're not going to get in. I had two-thirds of a pass and didn't make it.' The bishop was disheartened. However, he decided to carry on anyway.

He went up to the gate where St Peter was and said to him, 'I'm sorry, I've made a mistake, but I understand this is not good enough to get into heaven.' St Peter said to him, 'Well let us have a look.' He opened up the remaining part of the bishop's pass and it looked like this.

Figure 37

'Come on in, my son,' he said.

Could you create the necessary mitre by simply folding up the paper three times and tearing it? Of course, you couldn't. It's impossible. Here is how to do it.

Simply take the top left-hand corner of the page and fold it down flush to the right hand edge and make the crease, like so.

Figure 38

Then take the top right-hand corner and fold it down to the left edge, so.

Figure 39

Then fold it sideways, along the vertical axis (as follows) to make the Bishop's mitre.

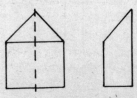

Figure 40

Try this now with a bit of paper, then make the tears in line with the story. You'll be amazed at how the impossible is possible.

Conclusion
The fit mind assumes that anything is possible. You just need to find out how. New ideas on how to make things happen are very powerful.

What Action Can We Take?
Feed your mind the food of the results of:

• the remembering exercise part one
• the remembering exercise part two
• The bishop and the thief

to focus it on finding out *how* you can achieve what you want rather than see it as impossible. Feed the food to others who limit you and show them how new ideas can be found to make things possible.

Barrier 4: 'Experience indicates that . . .'
Sometimes experience is limiting, as the following exercises show.

The Telling the Time Exercise
Check how well you can tell the time without looking at your watch. Do *not* look at your watch now, but guess out loud what time it is. Do it now. Now look at your watch. Double-check what time it is and call it out.

Now don't look at your watch again and without doing so, answer the following question: 'What is the number 6 on your watch (Is it a numeral 6, a Roman numeral, a dash, two dashes, a triangle or what)?' You have just looked at your watch, so surely you ought to be able to say what the number 6 is? Moreover, the average person looks at their watch up to 50 000 times a year. How long have you owned your watch? Some people have owned it for five years, so they will have looked at their watch about a quarter of a million times. As much as 50 per cent of the population, however, cannot tell you what the number 6 is on their watch.

The point is that, even though you've seen your watch thousands of times, by focusing on just telling the time, you miss something that is right under your nose. Try this exercise on others.

The Observe the Room Exercise

Look round the room you are in and notice everything in the room that is green. You have one minute and you're then going to shut your eyes and call out everything that you can remember. Look out for green. Look above, behind, by the side of you. Take one minute to do it, now.

Now, at the end of this sentence, shut your eyes and call out everything in the room that is *red*. You have just looked round the room, so you ought to have seen whatever is *red*. You have a smattering of answers.

Now open your eyes and look round the room and see how much there is that is red that you have simply missed. Try this on friends or a group.

The moral, again, is clear. When focused on looking at and searching just for what is 'green', you often miss what is 'red'. Typically, people looking for one opportunity may well miss other opportunities. People looking for what is wrong with a person, may well miss what is right with the person.

The Well-known Phrase or Saying Exercise

Can you spot a well-known phrase or saying in the following?

ASalTlsITCwHelIlNtThIatMeESnAdVEsSwNelINlE

There is *nothing* here that isn't *very* familiar to you in your previous experience. It is just presented in a way you haven't seen before. You are unused to seeing lowercase letters and capital letters next to each other in a way that doesn't 'read'. Spend a few minutes trying this before moving on.

Your previous experience will encourage you to try and read a phrase from sequential letters.

Now concentrate on just the capital letters. It's easy: A STITCH IN TIME SAVES NINE. You now have the right answer.

Focus now on the lower case letters: 'all's well that ends well.' Strangely, it's almost impossible to see both sayings at the same time.

This is another clear case of how easy it is to miss something right under your nose.

The Count the Full Stops Exercise
Quickly count the number of full stops on the next page.

There are two ways to do this: to read and count or scan and count. Try scanning and counting. It's easy and efficient. Do it now.

If you do this well, focusing only on the full stops, you will probably find you have read and absorbed almost nothing of the words. You have 'experienced' the page, but only *seen* the full stops.

How much of your current experience is really 'three years' experience of the job' or is it more accurately 'One year's experience three times,' or are you really not fully experiencing your job or your life at all?

The PIN Method
One way to help 'see' more opportunities and answers is use

the PIN method. For every situation or problem you face, assess it by identifying:

P: the positive things about it – these are the pluses
I: the interesting things – these are the things you notice that are not necessarily positive or negative, but may be influential
N: the negative things about it.

In assessing whether or not a course of action is the right one, some unfit minds will just see the pluses – particularly if it's their idea. A more fit mind will look for the negatives too, and weigh them. An even fitter mind will also search for the 'interesting' things and, by seeking and listing all three will arrive at the best possible overview. This will also produce the best chance for an even better answer.

What Conclusions Can We Draw From These Exercises?
The fit mind is prepared to look at other aspects of any situation to see how they might be helpful to them, rather than just relying on their experience – there are new ideas right under your nose.

What Action Can We Take?
Feed your mind the food of the results of:

- the telling the time exercise
- the observe the room exercise
- the well-known phrase or saying exercise
- the count the full stops exercise
- the PIN method

to help search for new ideas that will help you. Feed the food to others who may be limiting you by what they do not see in a situation.

Barrier 4: 'I know it doesn't work'

The Pike Syndrome

Put a pike in a tank with tadpoles and it will eat them up voraciously. Now put some tadpoles in a jar in the pike's fish tank. It will try and eat them but hurt its mouth and jaw on the jar. It will continue to try and continue to hurt its mouth. Eventually it will give up.

Now remove the jar and let the tadpoles swim freely in the pike's tank. The pike will not even try to eat them! No matter how hungry it gets – it may even die of starvation – the pike now 'knows' that tadpoles can't be eaten.

Ghosts Do Not Bleed

This is a story about a man who became convinced he was dead. He thought he was living as a ghost outside of himself. He received psychiatric help. One attempt to cure him involved getting him to repeat to himself for a month 'Ghosts do not bleed.'

He did this faithfully and then returned to the psychiatrist, who immediately got out a scalpel and cut his arm lightly. Blood flowed.

'There,' said the psychiatrist.

'There,' said the man, 'Ghosts *do* bleed!'

What Conclusions Can We Draw From These Examples?

Good mind-fitness is not letting yourself become so convinced about a situation that you cannot open your mind to a better solution or a more empowering point of view. Seek new ideas on how to make it work.

What Action Can We Take?
Use the mind food of the results of:

- the pike syndrome
- ghosts do not bleed

examples whenever you are so convinced that something won't work you refuse to even try it. Feed the food to others who restrict you from trying what you think will succeed.

Barrier 5: 'It is what it is; and things are what they are'

Limiting mind-sets can be started by anyone. Once started and supported, they can achieve an unstoppable momentum. When the boss starts it, it is particularly difficult to overcome. Prove it to yourself in the following ways.

Picture Exercise Part One
Draw the following picture for someone.

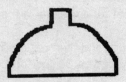

Figure 41

Describe the picture as a *stirrup*. Ask the person to leave the room and draw the *same* picture themselves. Then have *them* invite a friend in, show them the picture, tell them it's a stirrup and ask them to go away and repeat the exercise with someone they know, and ask them to carry on the chain.

Repeat the same exercise with somebody else, but, this time, show them the *same* picture and tell them it's a *bottle*. Ask them to go away and draw the *same* picture themselves, bring someone else into the room, tell them it's a bottle and ask them to repeat the exercise and so on, down a chain.

The next day, track the pictures through the chain. You will find the chain that was told the picture was of a bottle will end up drawing pictures like those on the left below, while the chain that was told the picture was a stirrup will end up drawing a picture like the one on the right below even though both have been told to draw the picture in Figure 41.

Figure 42

Picture Exercise Part Two

Figure 43

Tell one person this is a picture of a diamond in a square, ask them to draw it, pass it on and get that person to draw it, telling them the same thing and so on. Tell another person it is a picture of curtains in a window and ask them to draw it and pass it on in the same way as before. Similarly, the next day, track the pictures through the chains and you'll find that one chain has drawn it like the picture on the left below and the other chain has ended up with pictures like that on the right.

 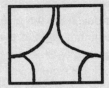

Figure 44

If you see only the end pictures you will conclude it is pretty clear what they are meant to be, particularly when you are told what they are. But the original picture was different. Passing through several people the picture changed.

Most of the time in life you are only seeing 'end pictures', not the original. Next time you see something that is unhelpful and you are told it is clear what it is meant to be, question it. Often you'll find out it was not meant that way in the first place.

Thinking Exercise

Consider the picture exercises the other way around. What is this you are reading? The obvious 'end picture' here is this book. Ask yourself the question 'How many uses are there for this "thing"?' and you will generate a number of answers. How many do you think you could think 5, 10? Actually you could now probably think of 50, 60 or even 70. Let me start you off. This 'thing' can be:

- a door-stop
- part of a series of weights to press flowers
- on its own, as a step to stand on to reach something higher
- pages as kindling for a fire

- a 'briquette' block as fuel for a fire
- something to throw at a cat
- something to put under a wobbly table to balance it
- something to put behind the wheels of a car stuck in snow
- a block under the wheels of a car on a slope to prevent it rolling
- an impromptu, spur-of-the-moment present for someone
- . . . keep going.

You will find you come up with more and more new ideas of 'what this is' thinking of it in a way you have never thought of it before. These are *new* ideas. This is a sign of a fitter mind; this is a sign of becoming creative.

What Conclusions Can We Draw From These Exercises?
If you are 'fixed' by an 'end picture' that doesn't help you to find a better answer to what you want to achieve, question it. Often it wasn't meant that way in the first place or isn't the only picture you could have of a situation or thing.

What Action Can We Take?
Use the mind food of the results of the:

- the picture exercise part one
- the picture exercise part two
- the thinking exercise

to question whether things could be another way to help create new ideas.

A Final Thought
The key to finding better ideas on how to get what you want in solving business or personal problems is to practise removing limiting mind-sets, changing them into more enabling ones and removing the barriers to new ideas that are often self-imposed. Enjoy the thrill of doing it.

Day 4

Good Mind-food For Snacks Between Meals

Snacks for the Body;
Snacks for the Mind

Mind-fitness, however, is not just the ability to remove limiting mind-sets and remove barriers to new ideas. What we achieve of what we want and how happy and fulfilled we are also depends heavily on how we feel, what our mood is. It's no good having the *knowledge* of how to find better ideas if we simply are too fed-up or too down to try; it's no good if we're not in the mood.

Mind-fitness is recognizing that our moods are caused by our own thoughts and the 'food' we feed our mind. Our mood and energy to succeed are dictated by our 'mind-diet' of 'mind-food'.

Most body-diets focus on what to eat, and what not to eat at any one mealtime. They set out a regime you need to follow. Often it's not very pleasurable. They also set out what you mustn't eat between meals – *no snacking*. It's the snacking, though, that we enjoy. It's probably the snacking that made us need to go on a diet in the first place. Thankfully it's the opposite with a mind-diet and that's why we are starting with the snacks. With a mind-diet the snacks are easy to do and a wonderfully satisfying part of the diet.

It's wrong to think of a mind-diet as consisting solely of some sort of early morning meditation, followed by a mid-day renewal of vows, an evening examination of conscience and a determination to do better the next day. That's one way, but it's hard and doesn't seem like fun.

The fun in the mind-diet is the snacking. The mind-food you can have at any moment, any time of the day, will dictate your mood and thus your energy and vitality to achieve the things you want to. It is 'food for mood' as well as 'food for thought'. Once you realize and experience the fun of this snacking, the other parts of the diet become easy. They are an extension of the happy snacking habit.

So, here is a random list of 24 snacks to feed your mind for each hour of the day. Eat them at any time, when you feel like it – it's like 24-hour room service.

24 Mind-food Snacks For Any Hour of the Day

Snack 1: When an Unjust Remark is Made to You

This happens often and really gets you down. You feel hurt, want to justify yourself in some way, but often don't get the opportunity. You want to retaliate. You feel down.

Instead, take the remark and imagine that the person saying it is drunk. Repeat the remark in your mind in a slurred, very slurred, stupid way. Intersperse it with hiccups. Do it out loud. Do it with a friend. Imagine yourself telling someone about it in a slurred, stupid, drunk way.

Doesn't that bring a smile to your face? Tell someone else, now, about this mind-snack. Watch them. They'll immediately smile and laugh.

This is a great mind-snack for wiping out an unjust remark.

Snack 2: When Something Unfair is Written

This can really annoy you. It's just not right, not fair. How dare they? You worry about what this might mean in the future and, as it's unfair and unjust, your value will be depreciated unfairly.

Instead, look at the comment with new eyes. Bring your head up from the table and look at it at a distance. It starts to look small. Imagine yourself floating up from your chair, still looking at the comment – it's getting smaller and smaller. Imagine yourself going right up to the ceiling. Wow, it looks really small now. There's no way you can read it. How small and insignificant it looks. That is truly what it is. Small, insignificant, unreadable. In fact, some spidery scrawl. Keep that picture of it.

Again, share this technique with a friend. Don't they smile?

This is a great mind-snack food for coping with an unfair comment.

Snack 3: When You Have Troubles

We all have troubles with our bad habit of remembering one thing negative and then remembering others. It's easy for our minds – once aware of one trouble – to remember all the other troubles. Life then just seems a real pain, almost unbearable.

Instead, sit down and visualize yourself writing each trouble down on a piece of paper. In your mind, put the piles of paper on the floor on your right-hand side. In your mind, get a box of matches, pick up the first bit of paper with a trouble on it from the top of the pile and set fire to it while it is in your hand. Visualize it burning and laugh. Imagine it burning right to the edge – ash flying – burning so that you don't know what to do with the last bit without burning your fingers. Mentally wave the flame out before your fingers get burned and put the ashy paper remains in an ash-tray by your left side. Then lean over to the right, and pick up the next trouble and mentally set fire to it and so on through the pile.

Doesn't that help put them in a new perspective?

This is a great mind-snack for when your troubles pile up.

Snack 4: 'Unlucky 13' and Universal Bad Feelings

Sometimes something happens that makes you feel bad, annoyed, frustrated or down. It's difficult then to realize that everyone else has similar feelings and about as often as you. It's human nature.

Indeed human nature only has about an 'unlucky 13' number of bad feelings in all – no more – and millions of us have them.

A good bit of snack food for the mind is simply to identify the feeling and name it. Here are the 13, in no particular order:

1 *feeling you're not appreciated:* perhaps your contribution is unrecognized, your worth is not seen, you feel undervalued

2 *feeling you're not listened to:* perhaps you are not understood, your view is not appreciated

3 *feeling it's unfair:* perhaps you are criticized unfairly or unfairly compared to others or unfairly treated versus others

4 *feeling you're unloved:* you feel others don't like you any more or are not concerned about how you feel

5 *feeling it's wrong:* perhaps something said or proposed or done is incorrect, incomplete, biased, inaccurate or just needs correcting

6 *feeling jealous:* like feeling unappreciated, but worse so as someone else is unfairly appreciated and loved more than you

7 *feeling humiliated:* perhaps you are talked down to, like a child, or have been corrected in front of others, put down in front of others

8 *feeling you're ignored:* perhaps you should have been consulted about something and haven't been or you feel

your contribution is ignored or considered not needed

9 *feeling overwhelmed*: out of control, rushed, no time to do things, too much to do

10 *feeling betrayed*: perhaps someone you trusted let you down, someone said they'd do one thing and did another, or perhaps you feel someone did something they shouldn't have done if they valued your friendship

11 *feeling envious*: perhaps you feel someone else has something you'd like – an article, way of life, luck, success, money

12 *feeling worried*: about what might go wrong, about a difficult situation you face or about something you have done, some mistake you have made

13 *feeling listless*: perhaps bored, lifeless, in a rut, tired, but not from doing anything, perhaps doing nothing, feel you're going nowhere.

There *are* only 13 and millions of people feel each of the 13 to some degree, every day.

The first piece of good mind-food for these is simply to identify which of the 'unlucky 13' you are feeling. Identify it. Call it one of the names above. Recognize that it's not the end of the earth, it's commonplace, will pass and, indeed, that you can *make* it pass and not overwhelm yourself, ruin this period of your life, nor even ruin your day, even this moment.

Second, give it a number 1 to 13, say, it's 'feeling number 7. Feeling humiliated', like a hymn number. Later, under Snack 9, you'll learn about the *good* feelings. There are 10, but these are numbered 100 to 1000. It's more fun to have these good feelings than entertain the bad ones and it's great to give them 100 times the weight, 100 times the power of a bad one. Call the bad feeling '7', but give a weighting of 700 to a *good* feeling.

Snack 5: Soap Opera Theme Tunes For the 13 Universal Bad Feelings

Recognize that each of these bad feelings is commonplace. In fact, this is the basis for the success of all serial soap operas. They depict 'everyday life' with characters and plots essentially tripping over one universal bad feeling after another.

Take time out to list all the soap operas with which you are familiar. Think about what happens in them. Plan to watch one tonight and identify the 'universal' bad feelings featured in it.

If you don't believe they are universal feelings, just consider how many of these soap operas can be shown on TV in different countries across different cultures. Indeed, how many of the ones you have seen are not made in your own country? Think how many pass the test of time and go on and on and on, for years.

Now – literally or in the mind – make a tape of the theme tunes of each soap opera. For British TV and radio, it might mean remembering the theme tunes to the following (note that they are not all British-made, thus illustrating the truth of universality of bad feelings):

- Coronation Street (British)
- Eastenders (British)
- Neighbours (Australian)
- Dynasty (US)
- Dallas (US)
- The Archers (British)

Include in your list, too, themes tunes of other shows that make you personally *laugh* at people's behaviour; perhaps game shows like Blind Date, or Wheel of Fortune. Now, whenever you hit a universal feeling, just play in your mind (or even literally on your tape) the theme tune of one of these programmes that seems most appropriate. Hum it, out loud – sing it. Doesn't that bring a smile to your face?

This is a great mind-snack for putting things into perspective when you hit a bad feeling. It reminds you it's universal. It reminds you to see it for what it is and not to exaggerate it.

Snack 6: It May Not be Real

Often our feelings are caused by some event or some remark that our minds interpret in a particular way. Once the mind has done that, we're into a 'mind-set' and the feeling persists. Probably, though, 90 per cent of the time, the event or remark *was never intended to give us that feeling*. Indeed, often, if the person involved realized the effect their action had had they would feel terrible and be contrite.

Most of the 'slights', the 'innuendos' we imagine are not really 'there'. Here's some good mind-food to remember through the day. Ten 'it's not real' pictures. Think how easy it is to 'see things that aren't there' in real life and just think how often this is shown in soap operas and, indeed, is a key part of their drama.

Picture Exercise Part One
Do you see a pyramid here?

Figure 45

Picture Exercise Part Two
Do you see a square here?

Figure 46

Picture Exercise Part Three
Do you see a triangle?

Figure 47

Picture Exercise Part Four
Do you see crosses, a square?

Figure 48

A circle, a diamond?

Figure 49

Picture Exercise Part Five
Do you see grey spots at the intersections of the squares?

Figure 50

Look at these pictures again in your mind the next time something happens to give you a universal bad feeling. Was it intentional or not or are you just seeing things?

Snack 7: 'Singing The Blues'

If the soap opera theme tunes didn't break up your 'down' mood for you, try 'singing the blues'. Search your mind now for a list of song titles that can illustrate 'your blues'. Remember the theme. In fact, make it a habit from now on to 'listen out' for songs with helpful themes for the future. Make a list of themes, along the lines of the following examples:

- sometimes you feel like quitting, so, at such times, sing in your mind Neil Sedaka's 'Breaking up is hard to do' – do it now
- sometimes you are troubled, so sing 'We shall overcome'

Similarly, identify song titles, like the following, and put them in your 'tape':

- 'I heard it through the grapevine'
- 'Baby, please don't let me be misunderstood'
- 'You're so good, you're so good. Baby, you're so good'
- 'I shall be released'

Make a list of 20 or so.

This is great mind-food to sing to yourself whenever you notice a 'blue feeling' coming on. Singing them out loud is even better. Singing 15 seconds of one is better than 5 seconds; singing 30 seconds of one is *very* effective mind-food.

Snack 8: Look at it From Another Point of View

For a great mind-snack, copy and keep the picture below. Leave it on your desk, around the house, pin it on a board. This is the universal picture for seeing things differently. Which long lines are parallel?

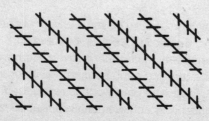

Figure 51

You will probably conclude that alternate lines are parallel and that there are two sets of parallel lines.

Now simply turn the book sideways, put your nose down on the paper and look along the lines. Look at it from another point of view and, hey presto, a different answer. They are *all* parallel. Who would have believed it?

This universal picture is great mind-snack food to help you remember to *Look at things from another point of view.*

Snack 9: Top 10 Feelings

Recognize that there are some great feelings that you enjoy. These make you feel great about life and, in turn, they help you be 'up' versus 'down' and get more things done, achieve more and bring more fun and happiness to you and those around you.

Recognize the following 'top 10' feelings so that you search them out and look into them.

Moreover, these feelings are given weightings of 100 to 1000 to illustrate their weight and value to you compared to the previous list of bad feelings, which are given weights of 1 to 13. Here, then, are the 'top 10' in no particular order:

100: *feeling you're appreciated and praised*

200: *feeling good about achieving something:* it's finished, completed, or a good result or doing something difficult, well

300: *feeling good about who you are:* your abilities, character and nature; feeling worth a lot yourself

400: *feeling you're motivated, inspired, committed:* feeling empowered, powerful, pumped up, buoyant

500: *feeling your work and worth is recognized:* feel people recognize your achievements, your abilities, your work, your contribution

600: *feeling active, keen, energized:* feeling you're looking forward to things, what will happen shortly, tomorrow, next week, next month

700: *feeling you're successful:* feeling good about what you've done in life, how good your track record has been, feeling you're winning in life

800: *feeling loving:* feeling good about others close to you, feeling good about who they are, what they've done, what you've done together

900: *feeling happy:* relaxed, satisfied

1000: *feeling proud:* of yourself or someone close to you

Snack 10: 'Top 10 Tracks'

Identify a list of tracks that can help bring some of these feelings to life. For example:

- a song that signals a special time for you and your partner
- 'My Way'
- 'Staying Alive'
- 'You're so good, you're so good, Baby, you're so good'
- the national anthem
- an uplifting hymn
- a team song, such as, 'Swing Low, Sweet Chariot'

Put these songs on tape – literally, and in your mind. Add to the list as you recognize other songs that help. For each of the top ten feelings, select one or two tracks that help you feel that way.

Snack 11: Choose a 'Fame Frame'

A 'fame frame' is a setting in which you can imagine feeling good about yourself. Put yourself in one of these frames to get the top 10 feelings. Imagine the following:

- *Newspaper article* 'Local person does well'. This article is about you. Imagine it, what it could say. Make up in your mind the most positive story it could be. See a picture of you illustrating the story. Write the article down in a notebook.
- *'This is your life'* You are chosen as the subject of a TV programme. Imagine the list of events that could be recalled. Imagine the list of friends and relatives who would be brought in. Imagine the good words that would be said about you. Write the list of people and events down in a notebook.
- *Sports superstar* You are in there, performing brilliantly. Imagine it, for a full minute or two. Hear the admiring commentary, the roar of the crowd, the rounds of applause. See the newspaper headlines the next day.
- *'You are the King or Queen'* Walk along through the crowds. See them waving and smiling at you. Hear the applause.
- *Guest of honour* Imagine what it feels like. See yourself arriving by plane, coming down the steps, the reception committee saluting, the red carpet. Inspect the guard and receive the march past from the rostrum, then walk to the Rolls Royce. The chauffeur opens the door for you, hear the soft clunk of the door shutting and yourself saying 'Home James', then purr off.

Snack 12: 'Set Some Positive Anchors'

Identify some people and events in your life that give you some of the 'Top 10' feelings.

- *'Cork board' anchor* Put up a cork board in your office or kitchen. Pin photos on it of people and situations that mean much to you, that bring a smile to your face or a feeling of love or appreciation. Look at the cork board photos literally or in your mind's eye. Change the cork board frequently (every two weeks).

- *'Frame and hang-up' anchors*   Frame certificates, letters, programmes, tickets or whatever that bring you top 10 feelings. Put them upon the walls around the place – don't leave them in a drawer where you can't see them as anchors. Put them around the office, in the bathroom, on the toilet walls, on the kitchen walls, in the coat cupboard. Look at them physically or in your mind.

- *'Memento' anchors*   Get the mementos out and put them in nooks and crannies. Don't leave them in the cupboard or an old suitcase. Go through the memento drawer now and the old photo albums and select some. In your mind, look forward to doing this.

- *'List of good qualities' anchors*   Take each of the people you care about or want to care about and make a list of their good qualities. Do it literally or in your mind. Include their good attributes, nice things they've done or said, good times you've had together. Write them down in your notebook. Imagine the person and recite in your mind their good qualities.

- *'Good memory' anchors*   Sit and think of all your good memories. List them. Not just recent memories, include childhood memories, big things and small things. Take each memory and give it a name, a label. Say the name and imagine the memory.

- *'Smile file' anchors*   Start a file in your office or desk of great results, congratulation notes, the 'well-dones' of life. Too often these are forgotten among the critical comments, the not-so-good results and the problems and queries. Actively *look* for things to file in your smile file. As a good mind-snack, glance through your smile file for a few minutes.

Snack 13: Choose a Pick-me-up

Identify the little things that cheer you up. It can be a simple thing like an apple, a cup of coffee, buying a magazine, choosing a new tie, wearing a different tie, choosing a different place for lunch, going for a walk at lunch, buying a tape, sitting in the sun, whatever.

Think of the last few weeks, of all the little things you enjoyed. Make a list.

Snack 14: 'No worries'

Still worried about what others think of you? *Don't* worry; there are millions of people in this world who don't care a damn about you – one way or the other.

Still worried? Listen, people are far more concerned with themselves than they are about you. Think of your funeral. How many people will come? The reality of life is that people would be concerned more about their own headache or their own cold than they would be about news of your death. That is a black picture but a real one. It's just how people are.

So, don't spend one second worrying about what bad things people are thinking about you. Most people deep down do not mind one way or the other, so don't worry.

Snack 15: 'News headlines'

Still feeling worried or down? Get it into perspective. Imagine your troubles being the news headlines tonight. Imagine the sound of the music for the nightly news, the chimes of the clock, then the usual, famous newsreader coming on with the news of you feeling down about this or that. Got it into perspective yet?

Snack 16: Laugh About it in The Future, Now

It's a well-known saying 'We'll be able to laugh about this in future'. This is the basis of a good mind-snack. The key is to say this and then add 'Let's laugh *now*'.

Snack 17: 'Focus on Afterwards'

Often we're faced with difficult problems or situations that we just put off and off. These are difficult things to do, which we know we *have* to do but keep on avoiding.

The good mind-snack in these situations is to 'focus on afterwards'. Feel the sense of relief and satisfaction you get when it's done. Even promise yourself a treat or a pick-me-up, but mainly focus on the relief. It's like jogging – focus on the wonderful shower at the end of it.

Give yourself the mind-food of associating with the afterwards feeling.

Snack 18: Recognize 'Splats'

Often remarks are made, almost without thinking, that put you down. They are not deeply meant, just everyday reactions and are typical in families. Call these 'splats'. There's a 'wife-splat', there's a 'parent-splat', and there's a 'social-splat'.

Feed yourself the mind-food of recognizing splats and calling them that out loud. Let it become acceptable behaviour at home, at meetings, at work, to say, with a laugh, that's a splat!

Snack 19: 'Buy a Gift'

Give yourself the good mind-snack of buying a gift for someone. Take the time to think about what you'd choose, what they might like and appreciate. They'll appreciate the gift anyway. How often have you even bought flowers or chocolates? Do you even know where the flower shop is?

Snack 20: 'Glimpse Ahead'

Give yourself the snack-food of glimpsing ahead to your loved ones. Picture each of them in your mind. Picture the small things: the feel of a hug, the kiss on her neck, the smell of her perfume, the smile of your child or your friend, even the friendly welcome of the dog, wagging his tail.

Snack 21: 'Smile More'

Eat the mind-food that if you just *act* better you'll *feel* better. Smile. Smile more. Smile at everyone you meet in the next half-hour.

Manipulate your face muscles. Unfrown your brows. Raise your eyebrows. Crinkle your eyes. Grin. Look handsome. Look seductive.

Act energized. Move briskly. Hop, skip and jump. Act happy. Act lively. Act vivaciously.

Give yourself the mind-food of knowing that if you act better you'll feel better.

Snack 22: Smell Some Roses; Pick Some Daisies

Remember a birthday. Get in touch with an old friend. Learn a joke. Look at the stars. Look at the birds. Look at the trees. Learn a card trick. Sing. Dance.

Snack 23: 'Mottoes'

Identify mottoes that help you. Write them down. Frame them and change them from time to time. Vary them. Give yourself the good mind-snack of reciting a motto and slogan. Here's a good one:

Notice where you are.
Look at what you want.
Choose it.
Move on.

Snack 24: 'Buy The Book'

For further great mind-food, resolve to buy *Your One Week Way to Personal Success* by this author (Thorsons, 1992)!

What Action Can We Take?

Good mind-food can be eaten at any time, unlike a normal body-diet. Indeed it's *best* eaten at any time – snacking between meals. Make a list in your diary of the following good snacks to treat yourself to during the day – one for each hour of this 24-hour room service:

1 when an unjust remark is made to you
2 when something unfair is written
3 when you have troubles
4 'unlucky 13' and universal bad feelings (write out the 13 feelings)
5 soap opera themes tunes for the 13 universal bad feelings (list your themes)
6 it may not be real (remember the pictures)
7 'singing the blues' (list your songs)
8 look at it from another point of view (remember the parallel lines picture)
9 top 10 feelings (write out the 10 feelings)
10 top 10 tracks (list your songs)
11 choose a 'fame frame' (list them)
12 choose some 'positive anchors' (list them)
13 choose a pick-me-up (list them)
14 no worries
15 news headlines
16 laugh about it in the future, now

Day 5

Good Mind-food for Breakfast and Social Occasions

How to Start the Day Well

How many different sorts of food do you give your *body* for breakfast? For a full English breakfast, it can be more than 20. Just imagine, fruit juice, cereal, milk, sugar, tea, toast, butter, marmalade, bacon, eggs, sausages, tomatoes, baked beans, mushrooms, fried bread . . . Of course, there are other choices for breakfast too – grapefruit, other fresh fruit, prunes, muesli, dried fruit and so on. Within these options there are different ways to prepare them. The eggs, for example, can be done in many different ways – scrambled, fried, boiled, poached. There is of course, a huge variety of cereals to choose from – you can probably immediately list 10 or 12.

There are, though, just *eight* courses of mind-food to choose from at breakfast time.

Course 1: An Easy Starter

Simply decide today that you'll eat some good mind-food to make *tomorrow* a good day *before* your breakfast tomorrow. Decide tonight to get out of the right side of bed tomorrow morning. Decide before you go to sleep how and why tomorrow is going to be a great day. Wake up on the run and energized, even before you sit down to breakfast. Try the following ways to give yourself a pick-me-up before breakfast:

- if you're showering, sing in the shower
- if you're having a bath, put bubble bath in it and have different one for each day
- use a facial scrub in the morning and a moisturizer to treat yourself – men, too

Course 2: Ideal Day

Work out what will make today an ideal day, then make it happen.

A great day is just part of what will make your life great for the next *week* or for the next *month*. In the chapter Day 7, Planning Your Mind-diet, you'll learn to work out what it is that will make the next six months the best six months of your life, the next month the best month of your life, the next week the best week of your life and so on to help find make today the best day of your life. What will make you feel successful and happy? Here is the four-step way to deciding this and making it happen.

1 Realize that success is a combination of both choosing well what you want and then achieving those things. The balance is important. You have to be able to both choose what you want and achieve it.
2 In choosing what you want, you need to consider every aspect of your life. What you want to achieve in work, in personal relationships, in leisure, in study and self-development, in your family relationships, in your marriage, sex and so on.
3 Realize that what you want to achieve over the next year or two may not be the same as what you may want later on in life or may have wanted earlier. (There are seven key

exercises to help you work up what you want. You can find these in *Your One Week Way to Personal Success*.)

4 Having chosen what you want – including considering your wildest daydreams – you then need to decide which of these are the most important to you. Which are the goals that if you are taking action to achieve them, will make you feel you are making progress towards being successful and happy.

5 Next, work out all the little things you can do that will help you achieve one of those goals. What is all the action you can take and which of these actions are likely to have the most positive effect?

6 Then split up those actions into little pieces that can be done day by day by day.

So, what will make today a special day will be to include in it some little actions that will help you achieve the goals you set out to achieve over the next week or the next month or the next six months. Even one, two or three small actions can help today be a very good day for you. They could be absolutely anything, like:

- writing a letter to enquire about a study course you've wanted to do
- buying a book on something you're interested in
- finding out about some travel arrangements to a place you're interested in
- opening up a deposit account
- deciding not to look for another job for at least a year
- going for a jog with the dog
- deciding to read to your child at bedtime
- choosing one night a week to be alone with your partner
- resisting biting your nails

Planning these little actions is the biggest contribution you can make to having a great day. Enter the little things you plan to do today in your diary and, tonight, write down the little things you plan to do tomorrow.

Course 3: Feed Your Mind Good Questions

Your morning could start with feeding your mind some really awful questions. When you do, just like in a mind-set, your mind will apply its wonderful powers to finding answers to them. Here's a diet of questions you can really go to town on:

- as the alarm goes off, 'It can't be this time already, do I really have to get up now?'
- 'Why on earth did I have so much to drink last night?'
- 'Why did I eat what I ate last night?'
- 'I wonder if the train is going to be late this morning?'
- 'I wonder if I'll get a seat on the train?'
- 'Will the traffic be bad today?'
- 'What sort of bad things will happen to me at work today?'
- 'What boring things are going to happen at work today?'
- 'How bad a day is it going to be?'
- 'What am I not looking forward to today?'
- 'What didn't I do last night that I should have done?'
- 'How far behind am I this morning?'

Instead of this course of bad questions, consider feeding yourself the following questions for its breakfast and getting your mind to work on their answers:

- 'What am I pleased about in my life today?'
- 'What am I excited about?'
- 'What am I enjoying and what could I be enjoying?'
- 'What am I proud of and what could I be proud of?'

- 'How could I make today one of the best days of my life?'
- 'How could I make today the best day of the week?'
- 'How could I make today the best day of the month?'
- 'How can I make today the best day of the year?'
- 'What's great about today?'
- 'What could be great about today?'

Course 4: Plan the Outcomes

As you think of your day, you'll realize that there are several people you're going to meet and be with during the day – from family to friends, work colleagues, people in shops, strangers, people on the way to work. Most of our days, we simply drift into these situations and the outcome of the situation is just whatever happens to happen.

For most situations, however, we can plan ahead what our ideal outcome would be and give ourselves mind-food to help achieve it. Let's take a few examples:

- if we're going on a car journey with the family, we know our ideal outcome is to have a pleasurable, fun and enjoyable journey with no rows, bickering, moans and groans
- if we're going to lunch at grandmother's, we know, similarly, the ideal outcome to have a pleasurable time, grandma thinking very highly of her grandchildren, proud of her son or daughter, thrilled to have received the family without the bickering, jibes, opening up of old wounds or unpleasant events that can often fester
- if we have a meeting with a colleague, we want them to leave the meeting feeling good about themselves, enthusiastic and keen to take whatever action we've decided
- if you have planned an evening out together, you want the outcome to be wonderful, fun time, that is going to be part of your future memories

Each and every one of our interactions during the day will have an outcome. Currently, without mind-food for breakfast, what that outcome is will be a mixture of fate, happenstance and chance during the meeting. It will reflect all the prejudices and preconceived mind-sets we have from all such interactions in the past.

Instead, at breakfast, decide the most positive outcome you'd like from two or three interactions during the forthcoming day. Set out to plan to achieve them. This will mean planning things like:

- how to approach certain subjects
- subjects of conversation to bring up
- how to change the subject if it goes down previously predictable well-worn paths that led to bad outcomes previously
- what activity to engage in – go for a walk together, go to the pub for a change, go to the park, take a walk round the block, go for a walk in the gardens
- plan your reaction when things start drifting towards the negative

One of the most frequent and important interactions each day is coming home from work. Planning the outcome of that interaction can be one of the most important things you do. The chapter Day 6, Good Mind-food to go Home on, is devoted entirely to this subject.

All during the day, there are interactions that are important to you, where there are very positive outcomes you could achieve that are far more positive than the ones you generally achieve. At breakfast each morning, give yourself the mind-food to think of the interactions to come and the wonderful outcomes you might achieve – and what sort of actions and attitudes you can adopt to achieve them.

Course 5: Eat Popeye Spinach

Popeye would open his mouth and pour a can of spinach straight down it. Immediately the big muscles bulged and he became very powerful physically. He did amazing things with his new-found strength. You can have exactly the same sort of mind-food as Popeye Spinach, that will empower you for the day, make you feel great, feel 'up', get lots of things done. Feed yourself this food for breakfast. Here are some examples of positive mind-food you can repeat to yourself:

- 'Today is the first day of the rest of my life. From now on I'm going to do things differently. I will get more out of life, more enjoyment, more fun, more achievements. I'm going to start this today.'

- 'I'll enjoy today as if I'm on holiday. I will have the same spirit and attitude as when I'm on holiday. I will look at others with the same attitude of friendship that I show around Christmas each year. I will act as though today is my birthday.'

- 'I really am unique. There's no one else on earth like me. I can walk the streets for several lifetimes and not see anybody who looks like me, sounds like me, nor is even close to the special combination of abilities that make me. I like me, I feel good about me and I'm getting better and better each day. I wanted to be somebody and I am somebody. I'd rather be me than anybody else in the world.'

- 'Nowadays life is very exciting. I'm learning more and more about how to be increasingly successful and happy. I don't allow myself to eat negative mind-food any more. When I find myself grazing on it, I simply pass over it to move on. I seek out the positive stations on my radio scanner. I don't allow the world about me to get me down. I am in control of me, no one else is – not others, not the world around me.'

- 'I know I've great abilities and I can use these to achieve anything that I choose to do. It is all a question of my attitude and my energy. Having the right mind-set is far more powerful than trying to change my mind. Just applying the power of my mind to help me succeed, helps me succeed.'
- 'Today's a great day. I feel great. I'm going to hit the day running with energy and vitality. I can get lots of things done and the more I get done, the more energy I have to do more. Today will be a super day. I will show interest and enthusiasm in everything I do and the more I do this, the more I will achieve, the better I will feel. I can make today a really great day for me.'

Course 6: Drink Some 'Spirits' to Decide to Get in a Good Spirit for the Day

- Put your favourite music on to start the day instead of the news.
- If you're driving to work, decide to let several people join the traffic jam ahead of you; give way and let them enter, with a smile.
- Decide to wave goodbye to the family as you leave. Decide to wave to children in the school bus. Decide to wave to somebody on the way to work.
- If you're in a hotel, decide to tip the morning waiter too much.
- Decide to compliment three people before 11 o'clock.
- Decide to make the first thing you say to each person you see be something that will brighten their day.
- Decide you'll find one small way today to improve your relationship with your partner.
- Decide to spend some money today.
- Polish your shoes.
- Decide not to criticize anybody or anything today.

- Decide that when your children or your partner hugs you to let *them* be the first to let go.

Course 7: Juices

- Polish your shoes.
- Decide to take out the rubbish without being told.
- Decide to change the toilet roll when it's finished.
- Decide to refill the ice-cube tray when it's empty.
- Close cupboard doors.
- Choose not to leave your clothes on the floor.
- Choose not to leave a ring round the bath.

What Action Can We Take?

Remember the courses – write them in your diary:

1 an easy starter – decide tonight how to make a great start to the day tomorrow
2 ideal day – plan and make it happen
3 feed your mind good questions
4 plan the outcomes
5 eat Popeye spinach
6 drink some 'spirits' to decide to get in a good spirit for the day
7 juices

Good Mind-food for Social Occasions

We often focus on food for the body to help on social occasions:

- 'Shall we have lunch together?'
- 'Please come round for dinner'

- 'Shall we go to the in-laws for Sunday lunch?'
- 'Can I get you something to drink?'
- 'Would you like a biscuit?'
- 'Would you like a cup of coffee?'
- 'Would you like some tea?'
- 'Please stay for something to eat'
- 'What would you like to eat from the menu?'
- 'What will you have for first course, second course, third course?'
- 'What wine shall we choose?'
- 'Would you like water? Sparkling or still?'
- 'Let's go for a curry.'
- 'Let's go to the pub for a drink.'

Far more important than this, however, is the sharing of food for the *mind* – it will oil the wheels of your social interactions far better than body-food. Social interactions and interpersonal relationships are very important to most people's lives. In fact, when people are asked in surveys which is most precious to them, safer roads, better environment, scientific advances, better relationships with their nearest and dearest and so on, relationships often comes top. The way to achieve great family and interpersonal relationships is to concentrate on *mind-food* to feed those relationships as much, if not more, than *body-food.*

Therefore, the next time you find yourself offering *body-food* for a social occasion, consider offering one of these pieces of *mind-food* as well.

The Parent/Adult/Child Model

Why is it that so often in our personal relationships we seem to get crossed wires. Sometimes we say something that is misinterpreted and some sort of row or problem ensues. The most innocent remarks are interpreted with a meaning that wasn't intended. Perhaps it *was* intended, though. Sometimes interactions just seem to be a series of codes and code words, code phrases. When coupled with facial expressions and body language, we'll react to the most simple requests or comments with anger, frustration or recrimination. It seems to be caused by a build-up of things over the years – 'You're always doing that', 'Why do you never do this?', and so on.

Here is a model to share during a social interaction as to why these things happen between you. Perhaps share the model 'just for dinner' not in response to any particular incident – choose a time when you're literally sitting down for food and, instead, have this as mind-food.

In each of us there is a parent, an adult and a child. At any one stage, we're operating in one of these three modes. We can switch easily from one to another and we can be in any one at any particular time.

There is a child in each of us waiting to get out. The child is full of fun and enjoyment, perhaps irresponsible behaviour, very creative and intuitive.

The parent in each of us is that part of us capable of bringing up children. We're able to teach them what is right and wrong, what they ought to do in certain situations. We do things because 'That's just the way they're done', 'That's what you should do' and so forth.

The adult in each of us objectively assesses all the data and reaches conclusions; it makes the calculations and the assessments that are needed to survive in the world.

Each of us, then, has a parent state, an adult state and a child state in which to start a conversation or interaction; and the other person has the same states in which to reply.

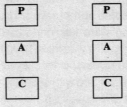

Figure 52

In starting an interaction with another, we have an expectation of what sort of response we want. It is when we don't get that response – we get a crossed wire – that the trouble starts. We expect these responses without really thinking or without really telling the other party what sort of response we expect and then we are disappointed when we don't get it.

There is no problem when the stimulus and the reply are in parallel. Thus, for example, one starts from an adult state, expecting a reply from an adult state along the lines of:

'Was there anything important on the news tonight?'
'Nothing much, except one minister resigned.'

This is an adult start and an adult reply, as shown below:

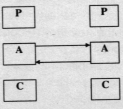

Figure 53

Similarly, there are no problems with a child start to a parent, and a parent to child reply. These are fairly typical:

'I'm not feeling very well at the moment.'
'Well, let me give you some aspirin and a glass of water.'

This is a child to parent start, and a parent to child reply.

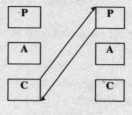

Figure 54

All the lines in the above are parallel; no wires have been crossed.

The problem comes when the wires get crossed. For example, the start can be an adult to adult start, expecting an adult to adult reply and, instead, the recipient is in a different mode. For example:

'Have you seen my pen anywhere?'
'Why don't you look after your things, you're always losing them.'

Here the start indicated the hope for an adult to adult response, something along the lines of 'It's in your desk drawer.' However, it got a parent to child response with the parent state telling the child off. The wires were crossed, as shown overleaf.

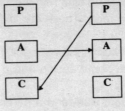

Figure 55

Alternatively, one could have had a child to parent response, along the lines of:

'Have you seen my pen anywhere?'
'I haven't touched it, honestly.'

These wires are clearly crossed, as shown below:

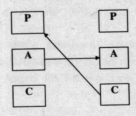

Figure 56

The reasons for these crossed wires can be many and various. Perhaps one of the parties is having some bad mind-food. Perhaps previously questions like 'Have you seen my pen?' have not been adult/adult, but have really been meant in a parent/child way, meaning 'You've lost it for me.' Perhaps one association is linked immediately with another association – a habit – such as, 'You're always leaving things lying around'. Whatever the reason, the interaction breaks down. It can only start working properly again by getting the wires parallel, somehow.

Share this model with each other and it will give you the mind-food to help get things right again. After a crossed wire, say something like:

'Sorry, I was after adult/adult and we crossed our wires' or 'I was just being child/parent and you came back adult/adult. Let's try again, can we?'

The important thing in all this is *not* to assume with each other that adult/adult is the best means of communication. It isn't. It is just one of very many. There is no such thing as 'be mature, don't be a child.' Do not use this model assuming that adult is better than child or adult is better than parent or parent is better than child – all of them have equal validity in our conversations. Each of us should have a parent within us, a child within us and an adult within us. It is the mixtures of all these modes that makes for a deep relationship.

By contrast, relationships that *just* exist in one set of parallel lines are normally fairly superficial. For example, if the only relationship that exists between a boss and a subordinate is parent/child and child/parent, then the subordinate is almost a slave. Similarly, continuous adult/adult is boring, probably lifeless and emotionless.

Next time you are oiling the wheels of your social relationships by having body-food, write on the table napkin the mind-food of the parent/adult/child model with those with whom you want to interact. It will give you a basis for even better interaction in the future.

The Bio-mirror Model

When you go to the cinema or theatre you often sit next to a complete stranger. The same on trains and buses. Sometimes, you can feel that you don't like that person at all. Sometimes the contrary happens – you get the feeling that you like the person; he or she seems sympathetic and friendly. What signals are you picking up to make these judgements?

The signals are the mind-food of bio-mirroring. If you want to seem friendly to somebody, the best way to achieve that is to adopt similar body postures to that person. Almost copy their body language exactly. This can even be extended to matching the pace or tone of their voice.

By contrast, if you don't want to be friendly to somebody, the easiest way to send out that message is to adopt opposite body language to them. If they lean forward, you lean back. If they open up their arms, you cross yours. If they are laid back, you are stiff and attentive. Moreover, if they are speaking slowly, you speak fast and staccato. If they speak softly, you speak loudly.

Share this model with your loved ones. It's not a way of being manipulative, it's a way of being welcoming and showing your empathy. Often when you're listening to your partner's tale of woe or concerns, you are, in fact, sharing that concern, but sometimes you just don't show it. Similarly, when you're telling your own stories or recounting your own experiences, you get the mistaken impression that your partner or loved one just isn't interested. The best way to signal your interest is to copy their body language, to bio-mirror them. It is a way of saying you're listening.

Try this mind-food with your loved one and ask that in future you each try bio-mirroring. It won't seem false – after a time you'll forget it's happening. If you *do* spot it happening, you can both notice it, comment on it, laugh and smile. When it *isn't* happening, you can tell your partner you're noticing it's not happening and are they really in disagreement with you.

This is a great piece of mind-food for the next time you're having a social interaction with your partner.

Find Out Your 'Love Mode'

Share this piece of mind-food with your partner. Each of us have different ways of wanting to be loved and having that love expressed. There are three modes of expressing your feelings and communicating them:

1 *the touching mode* – in love, this is to be hugged, to be kissed, to be held, to hold hands, to embrace, simply to be touching bodies as you sit together on the sofa, to have someone's arms around you in the cinema and so on

2 *the hearing mode* – this is to be told how great you are, how much he or she loves you, why they love you, all your attributes, all your beauty

3 *the seeing mode* – this is to receive things that you can see as an expression of how much you are loved, like flowers, chocolates, presents, cards, invitations.

Each of us, at different times, operates in each of these modes. At any one time, however, one or other is the stronger mode. If one partner misunderstands the mode the other is in, then you get crossed wires. If you try to communicate your love to your partner by *touching* when he or she is in a *seeing* mode, it will not work. Here are some examples.

'You don't love me, I know you don't love me.'
'I do, I'm always showing how much I love you – hugging you, putting my arms around you and kissing you.'
'But I don't like being mauled by you – you're always mauling me – but you never tell me how much you love me, let me know how much you love me. You're just always mauling me.'

Here what's happening. Your partner feels loved by being told you love them – the hearing mode. You are trying the touching mode and it doesn't work – it's viewed as 'mauling'.

'I don't think you love me any more.'
'Of course I do. I'm always telling you how much I love you and I do, I do. I'll always love you and I'm always telling you so.'
'But you never show me you love me by giving me flowers or chocolates or presents any more. I don't think you really love me.'

Again, the partner here wants love for them to be expressed in the seeing mode and you are trying the hearing mode. It doesn't work.

'You don't love me any more.'
'I do love you, I'm always showing how much I love you and telling you by bringing you gifts and telling you how much I love you.'
'But you never hug me any more or touch me like you used to.'

Your partner wants the touching mode and you are offering the hearing one. It doesn't work.

As a piece of good mind-food, work out with your partner what form of 'love mode' they are looking for at the moment. Are they in a hearing, seeing or touching love mode? Too many of us simply believe we know what our partner would enjoy and are actually getting it wrong.

This contrasts to the days when you were 'courting'. When you first go out with somebody, each of you tries every single love strategy to try and find the 'bingo' in the affair. Yes, you'll tell the other half how much you love them and you'll wax lyrical – perhaps even write letters and romantic cards. You'll flood them with presents and invitations. You'll also hug, kiss and hold them. You will vary the three approaches and gradually find out which one will work.

As a piece of mind-food, find out which one is your partner's favourite mode by asking them.

Work Out the 'Communication Mode'

In our social and business interactions, just like in love, our brains are operating between each of the above three modes – seeing, hearing, feeling. If we want to communicate well with somebody, we need to find out what particular mode their brain happens to be in at this time. If their brain is in a *hearing* mode, it's no good showing them something; if in a *touching* mode, it's no good *telling* them something. What is important is not what the person is doing literally, but what mode their *mind* is in. Here are some of the common everyday expressions that can help you identify what sort of mode a person's mind is in.

- *hearing mode* – 'That rings a bell with me'; 'That sounds good'; 'It rings true'; 'Sounds right.'
- *seeing mode* – 'That looks good'; 'I get the picture.'
- *touching mode* – 'That feels right to me'; 'That feels good.'

It is helpful to feed yourself the mind-food of working out what state the recipient is in. Let's take the typical example of a car salesman with a customer to analyse how this works:

- if the customer is really somebody who will judge the car by how it *looks* (seeing mode), then they will become impatient if they are held up in the office, being told how good the car is by the salesman, with all the details of its past history and its performance (hearing mode) – they'll want to get out and just see the car

- by contrast, if the salesman shows them how good the car looks (seeing mode) and the customer is really in a *touching* mode, they'll be resentful of the salesman's efforts to persuade them to buy telling them just by how it looks when, really, they want to get into it and give it a test drive to see for themselves (touching mode)
- similarly, if the salesman suggests a test drive (touching mode), but really the customer is in a *hearing* mode and wants to be convinced by all the attributes of the car and its past history and doesn't want to be 'conned' by a test drive lasting just a few minutes, then the customer will feel impatient and irritated at the salesman's pitch

So it is for each of the communications you take part in during the day. Give yourself the mind-food when you meet someone – perhaps just as they are asking what sort of body-food you'd like – of working out what communication mode they're in. How best will they receive your message?

The 'Walk with Mind-food' Model

Suggest going for a walk with someone you want to get to know, rather than just eating with them. With walking comes talking. Generally speaking, people walking together talk together. There is no one to interrupt them. There are no waiters, no format, no courses to go through, no social chit-chat. There are no niceties of convention to the talk on a walk. Moreover, the physical movement breaks down formality. It helps to break up mind-sets. It allows each person to 'let their hair down' a little. Walk with your business colleagues, go for a walk with your family. Walk with each of your children alone. You'll achieve more real communication than you ever will in a room or at the dinner table.

The 'Swap Stories' Model

Give yourself this great mind-food, to go with your body-food, of swapping stories. I'll tell you if you'll tell me. Here are some good examples:

- 'Would you like me to listen to you about your day and then listen to me about mine?'
- 'Why don't you tell me what goals you have and then perhaps I can tell you about mine?'
- 'Would you please tell me what habits I have you like and dislike and then perhaps I can do it in reverse?'

Decide at the moment of the body-food arriving to offer this mind-food to the social occasion.

The 'No Buts' Model

Next time you're having body-food together, give yourselves the mind-food of trying to have the rule 'no buts'. For the period of breaking food together, the idea is that no one is allowed to say 'but'. Every time 'but' is said, everyone should laugh.

Indeed, try also making the rule that nobody is allowed to disagree – everybody has to start off in response with phrases like:

'I appreciate what you say, respect it, agree with it. I also think . . .'

This is great mind-food for a social occasion.

Recognize 'Splats'

During the mealtime, say that you'll count the splats that come up and celebrate them in humour. These can be wife-splats, when something is said that puts down or criticizes the wife; husband-splats, child-splats, parent-splats. Make the word splat popular and enjoyable. Make it OK to ridicule it.

What Action Can We Take?

All the above mind-foods can oil the wheels of an interaction far better than can body-food. Make a list of them in your notebook as follows:

1 the parent/adult/child model
2 the bio-mirror model
3 find out your 'love mode'
4 work out the 'communication modes'
5 the 'walk with mind-food' model
6 the 'swap stories' model
7 the 'no buts' model
8 recognize splats

Day 6

Good Mind-food to go Home on

The Usual Situation at the End of the Day

Every day members of the family come home. It's not always easy to make a smooth transition from work or school or study or play to being at home. Also, those who have been at home need to receive the others home after a day when they've been away. Most of us practise the art of making this transition five days a week for most of our lives, but we do not often get any better at it. We rarely stop and think how we can make our evenings better for once and for all. We start off life adopting habits and practices that stay largely the same. We rarely improve on them. Whether we have a good coming home or a bad coming home seems to be a matter of chance and of mood, of happenstance and accident. Sometimes it's good, sometimes it's bad. We get into rituals and customs. We rarely evaluate whether they are good, effective or bad and ineffective. We just accept life as it is, that every day members of the family come home and it's a difficult transition that sometimes works well but more often doesn't work well. Often we blame the day we've had or the mood we've been put in by our time away from each other.

In fact, all this can be improved by better mind-food. We can give ourselves great mind-food to make the transition even better. Here are half a dozen bits of mind-food to share with your family to help make the transition even better.

How to Make It Better

Respect the Family

Most people who spend the day outside the home treat near acquaintances or even semi-strangers with far more consideration and interest than they do members of their own family. We learn to listen to business acquaintances to understand them, to empathize with them, to listen to their point of view. We learn to be polite and gracious to them. We even go on courses to learn how to interact with others better. Indeed, much of our energy is devoted to the art of working well with others, but we don't apply any of this to our own family in the evenings. We literally take them for granted. All the techniques we learn outside the home, we don't bother to apply within it. Within the home, we consider there's no need to try, thinking my family will understand. We just unload on other members of the family. Home is the one place we can really be ourselves and that implies that we are not going to try to get on with others. After all they're our family, they will understand.

The first piece of mind-food to give ourselves is to treat our relationships with our family members in the evening as being just as important, indeed more so, than we treat relationships during the day. After all, what does it really matter how well you get on with a trivial acquaintance compared to the fun, joy and happiness you can get from interaction with members of your family?

Entry Through the Door

Before you come through the front door, pause and give yourself some mind-food. Remember that the first few seconds or the first few minutes of your re-entry can create the ambience for an entire evening. A mismatch here, a lack of consideration, a mis-interpretation of your reception and moods swing, bad mind-sets set in and you repeat bad habits and bad practices from evening after evening in the past.

For example, he walks in, absolutely exhausted, but delighted to be home. She is busy, concentrating on something. She hadn't expected him home exactly at this moment, and her mind is elsewhere. As a result, instead of the hug he was anticipating, he got a non-committal grunt of a greeting. He decides he's not appreciated, gets into a bad mood and then storms off. She sees him like this, interprets it as resulting from something that has happened during the day and thinks it best to leave him alone. He'll get over it.

For all those entering home, give yourself the mind-food, that only *you* know the exact minute you are going to be arriving home, because you are the one arriving. The people receiving you are doing other things when you arrive – they do not know the precise moment of your re-entry. They cannot be there every second, laying out a big red carpet and the fanfare of welcome. The exact minute of arrival is known only by you. It's your responsibility to give yourself the mind-food to re-enter well, to anticipate that others will be doing other things when you arrive, and not to misinterpret the slightest signal as being a negative one. Don't get yourself in a bad mind-set because of the two or three milliseconds of impressions you receive as you come through the door.

Alternatively, she arrives home from work to find her partner relaxing, reading the paper or watching the TV, when there is work to be done. Perhaps there's washing-up to be done or the room is in a mess. She's had a hard day. She interprets this as laziness on the part of her partner, expecting her to do both a full day's work and do everything else around the house. The first few minutes of her entry have set up a bad mood for the rest of the evening. So the receiver can prepare in advance, to take out the obvious trigger factors that he knows may be misinterpreted. Give yourself some mind-food to think about how to make the re-entry positive.

When you come home, and you want time alone, just to unwind from the day, that's absolutely fine, but it's only fine after a few minutes of expressing how pleased you are to see each other, how great it is to be home, how great it is to be with each other again. This only takes a couple of minutes, after which you can take your time alone.

Call these moments the re-entry moments. For most of us they happen 5 days a week, about 48 weeks of the year. In all, 240 re-entries during the year. Aim to make your next re-entry better than the last and the one after that better than that. Aim, as a family, to get better and better at the re-entries, both making them and receiving them. Discuss how good the re-entry was. Ask each other what was good about it and what was bad about it. Get better and better at it, to give yourselves better and better evenings. Don't just take it for granted that re-entries are going to be a matter of chance or luck, whether they are good or bad. Give yourself the mind-food to address them and make them better and better.

'How Was Your Day?'
Again, this is a question that's probably asked about 240 times a year. Give yourself good mind-food to get better and better at answering it in a way that's helpful for all the family. Don't accept that how you answer it is just a question of mood and happenstance; plan ahead with mind-food. Here are some good mind-foods to help answer that question in better and better ways.

- *Give a short summary of the stories* Not the full details, just the top lines. Prepare these top lines before the re-entry. Say to each other you are just going to give the top lines and they are going to get more of the stories later. This is like just giving the headlines on the news at the beginning of the programme. You can always go into more and more detail later. Let each person give their headlines and have an understanding that you may go into them in more detail later.

- *Avoid the need for mind-reading* Don't require other members of the family to be expert mind-readers. They aren't and you aren't. If you're receiving others, don't sit there in a quiet mood or in frustrated expectation or with a frown or looking dejected and depressed and expect the others to interpret exactly how you are feeling and why. Similarly, don't go round, slamming doors, slamming cupboards, burying yourself behind a newspaper, slumping behind a drink. Don't leave people guessing what's wrong with mummy or daddy tonight. Again, in an edited form, label your feelings. Let people know what you're feeling and why, in just a headline fashion. A good arrangement to make is to say that there is no need for others to probe deeper or go into the story in a lot of detail. It is enough for each of you to just know how each of you is feeling without probing or prodding or discussing it. Recognize each other's rights to their own feelings, empathize with them, treat them as valid, say that you have recognized their feelings. Show through your body language your support and sympathy.
- *Be balanced* Before the re-entry, give yourself the mind-food of asking yourself two questions:

'What are the worst things that have happened today?'
'What are the best things that have happened today?'

Remember then to give *balance* as you give your headlines, rather than just reciting the one or two things that happen to come out of your mind because you haven't prepared with good mind-food.

- *Talking later* Decide when you are going to talk, when is the right time, and don't do it before then. Make a long story short. Don't give all the gory details. Spare them the blow-by-blow account. Negotiate how much time you should spend talking, say for five minutes it's your turn, then it is somebody else's turn. If there are problems in your day that you have already handled, then you've handled them – some things it is better not to regurgitate. Say you've sorted it out and you don't want to talk about it. If you're questioned, you are forced to relive all the bad things all over again. Use fun and humour as you recount your day, too. Share your techniques of using theme tune music, sound tracks that help, making things smaller, making things drunken. Impersonate others, imitate them to lighten things. Learn to choose words to describe the degree of feeling you have on negative things. Don't exaggerate and use hysteria or things will just get worse. On the other hand, feel free to use stronger words to express your positive feelings. For example:

  - describe yourself as 'mildly disenchanted' or 'annoyed' rather than 'furious' with something
  - describe yourself as 'puzzled' or 'disappointed' rather than 'let down'
  - describe yourself as 'surprised' or 'uncomfortable' or perhaps 'embarrassed' rather than 'humiliated'
  - describe yourself as 'a bit concerned' rather than 'anxious'
  - describe yourself as 'not on top of it' or in the 'lull before action' rather than 'depressed'
  - describe yourself as 'underwhelmed' rather than 'disappointed'

- describe yourself as 'fascinated' rather than 'frustrated'
- describe yourself as 'a bit bothered' rather than 'hurt'
- describe yourself as 'misunderstood' or 'misinterpreted' rather than 'insulted'
- describe yourself as 'a bit rough' rather than 'irritated'
- describe yourself as 'busy', 'challenged', 'in demand' or 'full of opportunities' rather than 'overwhelmed'
- describe yourself as 'overlooked' or 'underappreciated' rather than 'rejected'
- describe yourself as 'busy', 'energized' and 'active' rather than 'stressed'
- describe something as 'different' rather than 'terrible'
- describe yourself as 'miffed' rather than 'upset'.

On the other hand:

- describe something as 'great', 'excellent', 'dynamite', 'magic', 'brilliant' rather than 'good'
- describe yourself as feeling 'exhilarated', 'exuberant' and 'incredible' rather than 'great'
- describe yourself as 'peaceful' rather than 'happy'
- describe something as 'fantastic' and 'spectacular' rather than 'nice'
- describe something as 'perfect' rather than 'OK'
- describe someone as 'gorgeous' rather than 'attractive'
- describe the food as 'sumptuous' rather than 'tasty'
- describe yourself as feeling 'tremendous' rather than feeling 'good'
- describe yourself as 'replete' rather than 'full', 'relish' the food rather than 'like it'
- describe things as 'wonderful' rather than 'OK'

Learn to make the shades in between these words to help get the right balance in in your life. *Don't* use words that make you feel worse about the negative things than you did already; but *do* use words that can help you feel more positive about the positive things. Don't make things sound far worse than they are.

- *Don't respond with logic*   Give yourself the mind-food of realizing that often what others want is sympathy, empathy and the willingness for you to understand their feelings. They are not looking for a solution to a problem as they tell their tales. They are not looking for the events to be analysed, recommendations made and action taken. All they want is to be heard, understood and loved and then to move on. So, don't respond with these sort of questions:

'If you feel like that, I don't know why you just don't leave.'
'If you don't mind my saying, you really shouldn't have done that.'
'Here is what I think you should do in that situation . . .'
'You don't really mean that, do you?'
'What would be best is . . .'

Instead, empathize, say what their feelings are back to them and show consideration. This is great mind-food.

Anchor Before You Come Home
Before your entry, anchor yourself to the best things about your family. Let these run your mind, form your attitudes and so form your evening. Don't let your mind just drift around the first images of members of your family it sees as it goes through the door as it probably misinterprets these.
So:

- list in your mind all the great qualities of each of your children – what they do that pleases you, delights you, what you are proud of
- picture how they look when they are happy or satisfied or thrilled with a new experience
- list all the great qualities of your partner – the wonderful person you fell in love with; list how you would describe him or her as the most wonderful person on earth, what would you say in describing the thrill, the joy you get and have got from the relationship, what are the best things?
- picture your partner in the most pleasurable, wonderful, romantic way you've ever seen or imagined them
- picture the wagging of the tail of the dog greeting you as you come in and associate that tail-wagging with each member of your family; picture in your mind a wagging tail on each one – no matter how you might otherwise interpret the body language you're greeted with
- put a wagging tail on yourself just before you come through the door
- now you have set your mind on the good qualities, resolve to compliment each member of your family on something within the first half-hour of being home

Invent New Rituals to Switch Off Work and Switch On Home

Most of us have habits and practices to make the transition well, but they are so much part of the routine that they may have lost their effectiveness – they are dull and too well-worn. The old ones, therefore, may no longer work as well – things like having a shower, changing clothes, reading the paper, having a drink, watching the news.

Instead, invent new, vibrant ways to make the transition and that help others make the transition, too. Try different ones each day; change, experiment and invent. Here are some ideas:

- run or skip the last 100 yards to home
- drive the last mile at a very slow 30 mph
- throw the briefcase, like a shotputt, into the corner of the garage
- don't just aim to 'change clothes' – choose something bright, vivid, colourful to wear for the evening
- wear something different in the evening each night of the week
- sing a song
- go for a jog with the dog
- take someone out for a walk
- wave goodbye the office as you leave
- wave as you enter home; toot the horn
- ask others to think up new transitions for you or them to try
- plan at breakfast time the evening's fun transition
- play some music; pound the piano
- play a soap opera theme tune
- play 'our song'

Work to Live Not Live to Work

Decide that home is not the place you go to *from* work; work is the place to go to, temporarily, *from* home and leisure.

What do the figure 140, and the figure 225 represent? The first, 140, is the number of days this year that you will *not* need to go to work. That is, 39 per cent of the year! The figure 225 is the number of days, in addition to the 140, in which you will have about 14 hours in each day to spend on leisure and sleep.

Use the evenings to plan with your family how to make the very best of them. Don't let work dominate and the rest of the time be time off from work. Work is time away from leisure.

Plan the 140 days now. What would you like to do? Choose a time to do it. Fix dates. Agree a time. Commit yourselves – don't just talk. Always ensure you have a holiday schedule for the year. When exactly you'll take all your holiday, doing what, where. *Plan* the weekends, don't just leave it until the weekend arrives. Use your evenings to plan, agree and decide. Don't wait to see what happens, make something happen. Make this year's 140 days *twice* as good as last year's.

Plan the 225 days now. What would you like to do this year? How can you do some of it in your evenings? Vary your routine. Don't be a slave to timings. Never let yourself think it's all work and no play.

What Action Can We Take?

List in your diary or notebook the good pieces of mind-food to go home on that you have discovered here:

1 respect the family
2 entry through the door
3 'How was your day?'
   • give a short summary of the stories
   • avoid the need for mind-reading
   • be balanced
   • talking later
   • don't respond with logic
4 anchor before you come home
5 invent new rituals to switch off work and switch on home
6 work to live not live to work

Day 7

Planning Your Mind-Diet

How to Use What You Now Know

Now for your most important day. Up until now you have learnt little pieces of good mind-food, a smattering of good eating. You have probably eaten some good mind-food already and perhaps shared some with friends. With the help of the lists at the end of each day's work, you already have a 'menu' of good mind-food to eat.

The key thing now is not just to *know* about it, but to actually *'eat'* it well and regularly. Each week, on Day 7, you should sit down and plan your mind-diet.

For maximum benefit however, you need to avoid just 'nibbling' at it; you need to make the choice to change to a better diet. Change from that lousy mind-food you've tended to eat up until now to the great mind-food that can make your life happier and more successful from now on. You need to make the decision to change to a diet that will give you more energy, fun, success and fulfilment and which will help you bring joy and satisfaction to those around you.

Here is a list of good choices you can make *today* to make your life so much better, through a better mind-diet. Following this diet list is a weighing scale with which to 'weigh yourself' weekly to see how you are doing and what you need to do next week.

Choice 1: Choose to be Successful in Life
You are you, uniquely you. There has never been anyone

exactly like you before, nor will there ever be again. If you travelled the world for the rest of your life, you would not see anyone else who looks exactly you, let alone talks like you, acts like you, thinks like you.

Today is the first day of the rest of your life. Decide, from today, what are the things, big and small, that you'd like to do that will make the next year the best year of your life, next month the best month, next week the best week, tomorrow the best day. The choice, the exact balance, is yours and yours alone. Remember, most people spend longer planning their summer holidays than they do planning their *lives*. Learn to choose goals from all areas of life – social, business, study, material things, family relationships, hobbies, travel, sex and so on. Learn how you can take little actions each day that will help you make progress towards the goals you've chosen. Read *Your One Week Way to Personal Success!*

Learn how choosing goals – and taking small steps towards them – makes you happy and successful.

Choice 2: Choose to Run your Own Mind

You know already from this book the power of your mind and brain – you are learning to use it in better and better ways – but this is just a start. Remember, most people certainly spend longer working out how to make their cars run better than they do working out how to make their mind or brain work better. Recall that most power comes from how we 'set' our minds – the mind-sets we adopt – and choose to adopt empowering mind-sets versus limiting mind-sets. Recall that the power of your mind can run wild when it isn't you running your mind, when it is run by others or by haphazard events and signals around it. It's like the scanner radio that gets stuck on listening to the Hungarian programme because it just happened to pick up that signal.

Here are a couple of daily exercises:

'Turning the Knobs'

As we discovered in the chapter Day 5, Good Mind-food for Breakfast and Social Occasions, we represent things to ourselves in three modes – the seeing mode, the hearing mode and the touching mode.

We can, and should, run our mind by changing the mode of any representation to that which best helps us. In the hearing mode, we adjust a stereo for balance, bass, treble or volume. In the seeing mode, too often we remember something with a 'standard' picture intensity. It's like switching on a television and just accepting the picture that is produced. Here is a secret: practise turning the knobs on your internal 'TV' to get the sort of picture you want.

Remember the examples of words we use to describe the seeing mode:

- 'That looks good to me.'
- 'She has a bright future.'
- 'He has a dim and murky past.'
- 'He's a colourful character.'
- 'Put it behind you.'
- 'Don't blow it up out of proportion.'
- 'The outlook is black.'
- 'I can just see it now.'
- 'In my mind's eye.'
- 'It was under my nose.'
- 'She made a scene.'
- 'Paint a picture of that.'
- 'I take a dim view of that.'
- 'He's got tunnel vision.'
- 'It's clear cut.'

- 'I've got a hazy idea.'
- 'I see your point.'

Each of these phrases describes a sort of picture. You can and should alter the tone of the picture by which you remember things – don't just accept the first picture that appears on the screen.

For example, picture a pleasant experience. Now shut your eyes and:

- make it more colourful, more vivid
- zoom in on the subject of the picture
- make it clear cut
- make the picture last
- change it from a photo into a moving picture
- tilt the picture towards you

Each of these 'turns of the knob' will increase your positive feeling about that memory and bring a smile to your face. Don't accept the first flat, dull picture that comes on the TV of your brain.

By contrast, take a bad memory. Shut your eyes:

- make it black and white
- make it dull
- make it fuzzy
- put it at a distance
- make it a still photo
- tilt it away from you

Each of these turns of the knob will help put these pictures into perspective in your mind – tone them down, help you get the perspective *you* want.

Finally, return to the pleasant experience and associate yourself with the picture. Put yourself into it and be actively part of it. That improves the quality.

For the unpleasant experience do the opposite. Look at yourself in the picture from the outside, from the view of a TV camera, that is dissociate yourself from it and see it clinically. Change the knobs to get the perspective you want – fuzzy, dull, unimportant.

Learn to turn the knobs and dissociate from unpleasant pictures. Store them at the back of your mind, out of sight. Instead, *do* associate with pleasant experiences, make them better and store them at the front of your mind.

'Swishing'

To swish is to replace a picture of a problem with a picture of how you want to be. It's a way of running your mind in the direction you want to go. It helps apply the power of your mind to working out how to get there.

For example, say you want to stop biting your nails. First, picture what happens as you bite your nails. Notice what you actually see just before you bite your nails – perhaps a picture of a hand coming up to your mouth. Visualize a big, bright picture of the hand coming up.

Now visualize a beneficial picture. How would you see yourself differently if you no longer bit your nails? What would you be doing, how would you see yourself? Perhaps you'd be stroking your loved one and not being ashamed of but being proud of your nails. Perhaps you'd be delicately touching their face. Perhaps you'd be shaking hands or holding your hands up. Picture this.

Now swish these two pictures. Put the first one in front of you, big and bright, and then put your beneficial outcome picture, small and dark in the bottom right-hand-corner. Now, suddenly, explosively, let the outcome picture grow huge, bright and wonderful and push out the first picture, which becomes small, dark and back in a small corner.

Shut your eyes and do this five times.

You'll be amazed how often, when you next go to bite your nails, your mind will 'stop' the behaviour – you'll see the wonderful outcome picture if you avoid biting and you'll stop biting.

This 'swishing' technique can be used to run your mind the way you want in many circumstances. Simply:

* identify where you have a problem, the times you want to behave or respond differently and make a picture of what it looks like to flash up just as you start the problem behaviour
* identify an image of yourself if you avoided the behaviour – make it really appealing and wonderful, worth going for
* swish the second picture over the first

Next time, your mind will remind you of how good it will be if you *don't* do that behaviour.

Your mind does not have to be on 'automatic pilot'. How many times are we doing things that have bad outcomes without thinking. Get your mind to think for you; don't let it just drift.

Choice 3: Choose New, Better Ideas

Weekly, check your mind-sets. Review the week, review where you are and identify the mind-sets that are limiting you. Choose to adopt different mind-sets that help you get more of what you want out of life.

Weekly, check your barriers to new and better ideas and break them down. Actively seek new and better ideas in everything you do and enjoy doing it.

Loosen yourself up by changing set routines. Even put your shoes on in a different order to normal; change the order of morning ablutions; put your clothes on in a different order; drive to work a different way. Feel the freshness of the difference.

Think new, better and bigger. Feel free to challenge the world and then put the same sense of challenge in your own life.

- Why don't we announce that, from next January, we are cancelling Mondays. We'll have 60 weeks of 6 days each, each without a Monday. We'd still have Saturday and Sunday off and so get more leisure time. In return, we'd be prepared to work 10 hours on each of the 4 workdays each week. There will be 5 days over in the year after 60 weeks of 6 days. We'll designate these 'quiet time' between Christmas and New Year each year, when we each review the year we've just completed and plan to make next year the best year of our lives.

- Why don't we announce we'll *all* also change to working during the dark hours and have our time off when it's light? Then we can have far more choice of how to use our leisure time each day after work, whether it be fishing, golfing or gardening. There's no reason any more not to do this – most of us nowadays work under artificial light, even when it's light outside, and we can just as easily do this when it's dark outside. Let's do it from next January.

Choice 4: Choose to Change for the Better

Changing is a choice. We often make this choice in theory in our minds, but not with the right sort of mind-food to actually follow it through and make it happen. Here are a couple of exercises to help change.

Pain and Pleasure; Carrot and Stick

The reason we don't do things we intellectually want to do is because of the balance of pain and pleasure, the balance of stick and carrot, that our minds happen to associate with the action. If we choose to run our brains the way we want, however, we can question and change the balance of pain and pleasure we associate with the action.

Typically, we know we need to respond to a letter. It's a pain, though, to get up from the sofa, sit down and write it. It's difficult, unpleasant. It's a pain. It's a pleasure to stay stretched out on the sofa watching the TV, so we don't do it – we put it off.

We know we want to lose weight, but that chocolate will give us immediate pleasure. It will be a pain not to eat it, to go a little hungry. We eat it.

Every day, in many ways, the choices we make are based on the 'instant' assessment our mind makes of what will give us pain, so we avoid it, and what will give us pleasure, so we move to that. We don't stop and think enough about exactly how much pain we're in for if we don't eat the chocolate or if we do write the letter and how much more pleasure we'll get from being slim or getting that difficult job done. We don't stop and run our minds towards the choice we want; we simply react to the first 'instantaneous' assessment.

The better habit is to:

- give yourself all the mind-food of the good things that will happen if you *do* take the action – make a list of all the good things, imagine how much happier you will be, imagine the benefits of the accomplishment, make the reasons for change strong reasons, make them powerful reasons for changing *now*.
- give yourself all the mind-food of the pain you will have for *not* taking action now – make them big and powerful,

imagine yourself, negatively, in the old habit you want to change.

By realizing and imagining all the pain you can incur by *not* doing something you want to do and reinforcing in your mind all the pleasure you can get from doing it, you help yourself change for the better. Don't make the decision to change or not a function of the first, immediate assessment that comes into your mind.

Change Beliefs

All of us have beliefs that limit us. The belief becomes a mind-set and a different action becomes difficult, if not impossible. Our convictions limit us.

Change the conviction, mind-set or belief, however, and you become empowered to change.

For example, list now some areas of your life with which you are dissatisfied. For these, write down the basic assumption or belief you have that is restricting you. Pick something that would make a real difference to you if your belief was different, for example:

- we *have* to live in England
- I *can't* change my job
- my routine is *fixed*
- I *don't* like Mrs so and so

Give yourself the mind-food of adopting an alternative belief that would free your choices and your action. State your new belief in positive terms.

Now run your mind yourself by swishing pictures of your new belief to replace the old limiting one.

This will focus your mind on opportunities that will come from change, rather than on the mind-sets that mean you can't.

Choice 5: Choose Not to Become Stuck

All of us become stuck, but each of us can use good mind-food to move on. Staying stuck is simply the outcome of not feeding ourselves the food to move on. Choosing not to become stuck in the first place is to choose mind-food to help us move on. Try the following:

Avoid the Trap of 'Rite' and 'Rong'

In many things, there is no right and wrong, only 'rite' and 'rong', the imposters of truth.

Certainly in science there tends to be right and wrong. Our minds can sort these out. Thus, we can go to the moon, invent portable phones, build superb computers, build planes to travel at the speed of sound. At the same time, we can't solve the social and religious problems of Northern Ireland; nor the problems of racial discrimination, of behaviour patterns to prevent the spread of Aids – we find it easier to solve the problem of finding a miracle drug.

The reason is that in these situations there is less right and wrong, more 'Rite and Rong'.

Without good mind-food we can convince ourselves something is right when it really isn't. It's half right – just rite. Typically, in conversations and discussions we adopt a position and then use our minds to find all the supporting arguments and data as to why it is right. Often we confuse this with being 'clever'. It really isn't clever, it's being 'stuck'.

Good mind-food is remembering that, outside science, most things are not right and wrong; we just let our minds think they are. Remember instead the terms 'rite' and 'rong' and take a different mind-track.

Ask for What you Want

Don't become stuck by expecting others to be mind-readers.

'I shouldn't have to ask', 'If they were thinking considerately of me, they would do this automatically', we say.

Don't become stuck in this way. Simply ask, 'How would you like to do this for me? It would make me really happy.'

Choice 6: Choose to Have Positive Anchors in Your Life

Choose to fall in love again. Choose to associate with all the good things about your partner. Choose to remember the great things about you and your life. Revisit them. Associate with them. Choose to identify and remember the positive sides about each person you come in contact with. Choose good self-talk to feed to yourself as good mind-food.

Choose to associate with those good ritual feelings that come at Christmas time, your birthday, when you're in a holiday mood. Today, choose to have a Christmas feeling, a birthday feeling, an on-holiday feeling.

Choice 7: Choose to Put Your Mind-Food Diet Plan in a Diary

Go through this book and complete each of the exercises that have been set. List the summaries at the back of a diary.

Each day, plan what to eat as mind-food in the same way as you consider what to eat as body-food.

The Weekly Weighing

There are 83 questions beginning on the next page. Copy them and, each week, tick whether you have or have not eaten that particular mind-food or done that particular exercise. Keep your score. Aim to increase it week by week.

This week I have or have not	Have	Have Not
·1 I have shared the 'see' something pictures with new people.		
2 I have frequently thought of what mind-food to have when I've thought of body-food.		
3 I have reduced acting closed-minded.		
4 I have reduced accepting that there can't be a better idea.		
5 I have reduced the habit of 'grazing'.		
6 I have reduced the habit of having a bad day.		
7 I have reduced once remembering one bad thing, remembering others.		
8 I have reduced allowing the wrong frame of reference.		
9 I have reduced predictably slipping into negative behavioural patterns.		
10 I have reduced perpetuating bad mind-sets.		
11 I have reduced feeding my mind the wrong questions.		
12 I have reduced focusing on minor things.		
13 I have moved from having a fixed mind to having a flexible mind.		

This week I have or have not	Have	Have Not
14 I have shared the mind-set exercises with others (silk, toast, sign language, fine night tonight, car crash).		
15 I have seen the other point of view and got others to see mine using the old lady/young lady; eskimo/red indian; and 13/B.		
16 I have used E, Jesus Christ and dalmatian pictures to learn not to reject suggestions out of hand.		
17 I have checked whether facts are really facts when they limit me and used right angles, triangles, imperfect circles and unstraight lines, rows of dots, famous phrase, footstep, A bigger than B and A, F, 3, 2 pictures and exercises.		
18 I have looked for better answers using squares, joining nine dots, IX into 6, remove six letters, rows of glasses, birthdays and recognizing mother exercises.		
19 I have avoided restricting patterns using anagram solutions, days in month, I before E and QWERTY exercises.		

This week I have or have not	Have	Have Not
20 I have avoided 'It's not possible' using 10 objects, 52 cards and the bishop and the thief exercises.		
21 I have avoided 'experience' limiting me, using telling the time, observe the room, well-known phrase, count the full stops exercises and the PIN method.		
22 I have avoided the barrier 'knowing it won't work' using the pike syndrome and ghosts do not bleed exercise.		
23 I have avoided being limited by end-pictures using stirrup/bottle, curtains and book as a thing exercises.		
24 I have used the snack 'When an unjust remark is made'.		
25 I have used the snack 'When something unfair is written'.		
26 I have used the snack 'When you have troubles'.		
27 I have referred to the list of 13 bad feelings.		
28 I have sung a soap opera theme tune often.		
29 I have developed a new extra soap opera for my repertoire.		

This week I have or have not	Have	Have Not
30 I have shared the pictures of 'It may not be real'.		
31 'Sung the blues'.		
32 I have developed a new song for my repertoire.		
33 I have shared the parallel lines picture for a new point of view.		
34 I have referred to the list of top 10 feelings.		
35 I have listed my top 10 tracks.		
36 I have added a new top 10 track.		
37 I have used the fame frames, newspaper article, this is your life, sports superstar, you are the King or Queen and guest of honour.		
38 I have used the positive anchors, cork board, frame and hang-up, mementos, list of good qualities, good memory and smile file.		
39 I have used pick-me ups.		
40 I have used the 'no worries' snack.		
41 I have used the news headlines snack.		
42 I have used 'laugh about it in the future, now' snack.		

This week I have or have not	Have	Have Not
43 I have focused on afterwards.		
44 I have recognized splats.		
45 I have bought a gift.		
46 I have glimpsed ahead.		
47 I have smiled more.		
48 I have smelt more roses, picked more daisies.		
49 I have used mottoes.		
50 I have referred to the book *Your One Week Way to Personal Success*.		
51 I have decided the night before to get a great starter to the next day.		
52 I have planned my ideal day at breakfast.		
53 I have fed my mind good mind-food questions at breakfast.		
54 I have planned the outcomes of the day.		
55 I have given myself popeye spinach.		
56 I have used the good spirit mind-food for breakfast.		
57 I have used the breakfast juices to get me going.		
58 I have shared the parent/adult/child model for social occasions.		

This week I have or have not	Have	Have Not
59 I have used bio-mirroring and shared it.		
60 I have shared the love mode model.		
61 I have shared thinking, hearing, feeling modes.		
62 I have used the walk with mind-food model.		
63 I have used the swap stories model at social occasions.		
64 I have shared the no buts model at social occasions.		
65 I have shared the recognize splats model.		
66 I have used the respect the family idea for coming home mind-food.		
67 I have each night worked out the entry through the door mind-food.		
68 I have used the how was your day techniques – short summary, avoiding the need for mind-reading, being balanced, talking later, no logic, anchor before.		
69 I have anchored before coming home.		
70 I have invented new rituals for transitions.		
71 I have planned the 140 and 225 days.		

This week I have or have not	Have	Have Not
72 I have chosen this week to be successful in life, chosen what I want and taken action towards it.		
73 I have chosen to run my own mind – used turning the knobs.		
74 I have used swishing regularly to run my own mind.		
75 I have chosen to have new, better ideas.		
76 I have changed pain/pleasure balance to achieve progress.		
77 I have changed beliefs, actively.		
78 I have chosen to avoid 'Rite'/'Rong' traps.		
79 I have checked my mind-sets.		
80 I have asked for what I want.		
81 I have chosen positive anchors.		
82 I have used my mind-food diet plan in a diary.		
83 I have spent 30 minutes on my weekly weighing and planning my mind-diet.		

Today is the first day of the rest of your life, so enjoy it!

Of further interest . . .

Your One Week Way to Personal Success
John O'Keeffe

Your One Week Way to Personal Success is a simple yet powerful method of creating profound and long-lasting success in every area of your life. It works no matter who you are, what you do or how old you are. And it can be put into practice in just a week.

Find out how to make next week the best week of your life, next month the best month and next year the best year! In one week you will learn techniques for managing your life, yourself and others around you. You will discover what it is you really want to achieve and will have formulated an action plan to get it. And if all you have now is just a vague sense that you want more out of life, here are hundreds of ideas to inspire you.

John O'Keeffe has used this infallible method to achieve extraordinary personal success. He became a hockey international at 19 and his own boss at 21. He taught himself Mandarin, has travelled all over the world and at 38 became managing director of a world famous company.

Give yourself a week to find out what his system can do for you!

Bring Out the Magic in your Mind

The worldwide bestseller that can launch you on the road to success

Al Koran

Amazing mental powers already exist in your own mind! They can be harnessed to bring you prosperity, success, health and vitality. The secret of getting in touch with these powers is stillness. In the increasingly noisy world we live in, stillness and silence are the route to our subconscious mind.

Al Koran baffled common sense and science with his astonishing ability to read minds, predict the future and reveal the contents of sealed boxes. Here he discloses the powers that will enable you to take charge of your destiny, call riches to you like a magnet, and help you to achieve success and happiness.

You Can Feel Good Again

The good news about depression

Richard Carlson

Many cures for depression have been proposed over the years. Nearly all of them have said it is necessary to explore in depth the sufferer's negative feelings and past trauma. And most of them have failed. Now a radical new approach suggests a much simpler solution, one that is within everyone's grasp without the need for professional help. You can feel good again if you grasp that:-

- your thoughts determine the way you feel
- thinking about problems only makes them worse
- thinking is not something that happens to you, but something you do to create your experience
- thoughts you produce when you're unhappy are inevitably negative and therefore not to be trusted
- thoughts come and go – you're free to choose at any moment which you hold on to and which you let go of
- you can learn to dismiss negative thoughts and find inner contentment.

Recommended by doctors and therapists, including Waynne Dyer and Gerald Jampolsky, Richard Carlson's simple yet direct approach offers a realistic route away from depression – towards happiness.

Take Charge of your Life

How not to be a victim

Louis Proto

Do you ever feel:

- trapped
- helpless
- under pressure
- resentful?

If your answer is 'very often' or 'all the time', you could well be caught in the victim trap without knowing it.

It's not life that make us victims, but how we perceive it. By becoming aware of how we get into the victim trap we can escape before it snaps shut. In *Take Charge of your Life*, well-known psychologist Louis Proto shows us that more often than not we can choose our reaction to what happens to us. Handing us the tools of analysis and support – including visualization, relaxation and meditation – he explains how we can use our experiences to grow and become more whole.

Taking time and space for ourselves, creating more harmonious relationships, and emerging from financial and emotional pressures can all be achieved by learning how to become aware of our own needs and get back the power we have given away. Once we take responsibility for our own experiences, we can use our energy to create the quality of life we want for ourselves.

Who's Pulling your Strings?

How to stop being manipulated by your own personalities

Louis Proto

Have you ever wondered why you act the way you do? Why, for example, did you choose your job or partner? Why do you like or dislike certain people, attract certain experiences, even keep repeating the same patterns?

What we call our 'character' or our 'nature' is a mixture of different personalities, an 'inner family', each with its own life story, emotions and philosophy – and each takes its turn pulling our strings. Our Inner Critic, for example, tells us we're not good enough, while our Pleaser will make us do anything to keep others happy, even though our Warrior is ready to confront anyone.

By becoming aware of these often hidden personalities, and understanding their influence, we can work towards achieving inner harmony. As we become more comfortable with any parts of ourselves we may have condemned as 'bad' or 'ugly', we will also be less inclined to feel threatened or judgemental when these traits appear before us in others. Here, using some of the techniques and theories of psychotherapy, psychologist Louis Proto shows how we can begin to explore our own selves and learn to pull our own strings.

YOUR ONE-WEEK WAY TO PERSONAL
  SUCCESS   0 7225 2599 0   £4.99   ☐
BRING OUT THE MAGIC IN YOUR MIND   0 7225 2969 4   £5.99   ☐
YOU CAN FEEL GOOD AGAIN   0 7225 2867 1   £5.99   ☐
TAKE CHARGE OF YOUR LIFE   0 7225 2869 8   £5.99   ☐
WHO'S PULLING YOUR STRINGS?   0 7225 2870 1   £5.99   ☐
PRESS PAUSE ON YOUR LIFE   0 7225 2848 5   £4.99   ☐
THE SUCCESS SYSTEM THAT NEVER FAILS   0 7225 2228 2   £5.99   ☐

All these books are available from your local bookseller or can be ordered direct from
the publishers.

To order direct just tick the titles you want and fill in the form below:

Name: _____
Address: _____
_____
_____ Postcode: _____

Send to: Thorsons Mail Order, Dept 3, HarperCollins*Publishers*, Westerhill
Road, Bishopbriggs, Glasgow G64 2QT.
Please enclose a cheque or postal order or your authority to debit your
Visa/Access account —

Credit card no: _____
Expiry date: _____
Signature: _____

— up to the value of the cover price plus:
UK & BFPO: Add £1.00 for the first book and 25p for each additional book
ordered.
Overseas orders including Eire: Please add £2.95 service charge. Books
will be sent by surface mail but quotes for airmail despatches will be given
on request.

24 HOUR TELEPHONE ORDERING SERVICE FOR ACCESS/VISA
CARDHOLDERS — TEL: **041 772 2281.**